Day of the Lamb

Edgar C. James

This book is designed for your personal reading pleasure and profit. It is also designed for group study. A leader's guide with helps and hints for teachers and visual aids (Victor Multiuse Transparency Masters) is available from your local bookstore or from the publisher.

VICTOR BOOKS

a division of SP Publications, Inc.

WHEATON. ILLINOIS 60187

Offices also in Fullerton, California • Whitby, Ontario, Canada • Amersham-on-the-Hill, Bucks, England

Second printing, 1980

Unless otherwise noted, Scripture quotations are taken from the King
James Version. Other quotations are from the (NASB), © 1960, 1962,
1963, 1968, 1971, 1973 by The Lockman Foundation, La Habra, California; and the *New International Version* (NIV), © 1978 by The New
York International Bible Society. All quotations used by permission.

Library of Congress Catalog Card Number: 79-92804
ISBN: 0-88207-793-7

VICTOR BOOKS
A division of SP Publications, Inc.
P. O. Box 1825 • Wheaton, Illinois 60187

Contents

To my daughters
Sharon and Brenda
who have taught me much
about life, love, and the Lamb

1
Who
Is
Jesus
Christ?

(Revelation 1)

It's getting louder and louder! The cry for solutions to the world's problems is getting louder. In fact, it is rapidly becoming a crescendoing shriek.

Years ago visionaries looked beyond the problems to possible solutions. "But now," as one business leader told me, "everywhere I look the crises are overwhelming. I keep putting my fingers in the dikes, but the crises keep coming."

Crises? What crises? A woman in her 30s shared hers with me. "I always dreamed I would marry the perfect man," she said, "but today my marriage is anything but perfect. My husband left me when I was pregnant with my third child, and after two years alone I'm at the end of my rope. Where can I go for help? I don't see any possible solution."

A businessman told me of his problem. "Inflation is about to eat me up," he said. "My brother and I began our business 10 years ago, and it looked like a good thing for awhile. But now with rising prime rates, regulations, and escalating wages, things are turning sour. I think we can hang on for a few more months, but then it looks like we'll be over the deep end. I don't know where I can turn for help.''

World leaders, as well as families and business people, also see problems. Donald Rumsfeld, once U.S. Secretary of Defense, recently said, "There is a fundamental instability in the world." And this instability is seen in the world struggle in China, the search for identity in Africa, and in the distribution of energy from the Middle East.

Energy, the strategic problem of our day, is causing the greatest redistribution of wealth in the history of the world. Suddenly, the oil-consuming nations are at the mercy of the oil-producing nations, and this is having vast economic, political, and military effects. Whoever controls the oil of the Middle East controls the energy source of the world. And the nations of the earth are competing for this increasingly scarce commodity.

Even though the world has problems on every hand, things are not as bad as they could be. Oil supplies could be shut off completely. Earthquakes could be causing world devastation. Wars could be annihilating whole countries. A dictator could be running the world and attempting to destroy it.

We live in a day of uncertainty, a day of unrest. While general instability increases, we rush to do things this year because there may not *be* a next year. Yet the real question we must ask ourselves is this: *Is there any lasting solution to the problems we face? Is there any way out of this mess?*

Every generation has dreamed of a time and place when there would be no more war and everything would be all right. The early philosopher Plato, in his *Republic*, dreamed of a time of peace and world prosperity. Arab legends described an earthly paradise in the Atlantic Ocean. In 1516 Sir Thomas More wrote of Utopia, an ideal commonwealth whose inhabitants would live under perfect conditions.

All of these are inferior hopes, however, when compared with the greatest book on prophecy ever written, the last book in the Bible—the Book of Revelation. This book describes how the world's problems will grow worse and worse, how vast judgments will be poured out upon the earth, and yet how one day there will be world peace. Its message is that there is a great day coming!

The Book of Revelation's theme is the Man who descends through the sky on a white horse with the eyes of the world riveted to Him. Great armies follow as judgment takes place on the earth. Suddenly, as if a gigantic atom is split, the world is changed. It is then that righteousness prevails throughout the world. It is then that nations do not lift up swords against each other. It is then that there is a new world order, a new economic system, a new administration of justice. It is then that there is lasting peace on earth.

In order to understand the Book of Revelation we must start at the beginning. We must see who wrote it and why. By discovering its purpose and teaching, we can apply its truths to our lives. Then, as we are changed by its teaching, we will be able to deal with the world problems we are facing. What, then, is the subject of the first chapter?

The Preface [1:1-3]

In this first paragraph, the writer reveals the purpose of the book, the author of the book, and the blessing for the reader. Notice the key words of each of the first three verses.

Revelation (1:1). Books of the Bible get their names in different ways. Some books are named for the people to whom they are addressed (e.g., Romans, Corinthians, Galatians, Ephesians). Other books are named for their human authors (e.g., Matthew, Mark, Luke, John). But some books get their names from the first words of that particular book. This is true with the first book in the Bible (Genesis means "beginning") and the last book, the Book of Revelation.

What does the word *revelation* mean? It means to unveil, uncover, or disclose. This book is the revelation from Jesus Christ, for it was God who gave this message to John. But it also is the unveiling of Jesus Christ as the coming Judge and King of the earth. The central theme of biblical prophecy is not Israel, the Gentiles, the church, or the Antichrist, as important as these are. The central theme is Jesus Christ Himself.

Record (v. 2). Some have tried to make the symbols and figures of this book mean most anything. But careful study shows these symbols and figures are interpreted by the passages themselves, and God is teaching truth to be obeyed by us today. All of the Revelation is declared to be "the Word of God," and John is writing by the guidance of the Holy Spirit (cf. 2 Peter 1:21). You and I may not always understand the meaning of a particular passage, but that in no way affects the fact each passage is from God.

Read (v. 3). Any book of Scripture is profitable for us to study, but this book has a special blessing for those who read, hear, and heed the words of this prophecy. I know people who will travel 100 miles to hear a great preacher, but won't walk across their living room to read the last book of the Bible. God wants us to live in the light of the great hope we have in Him. And when we do, it will have a purifying effect on us. This fact is so important it is repeated in the 22ND Chapter of Revelation (22:7).

The Persons [1:4-8]

John (1:4a). The Apostle John wrote the Book of Revelation to the seven churches in Asia Minor, the Roman province which is now part of modern Turkey. John is the human author of five books of Scripture (The Gospel of John, 1 John, 2 John, 3 John, and the Book of Revelation). The churches mentioned are the seven churches named in verse 11 and described in chapters 2 and 3.

The Father (v. 4b). Since the message is from God, however, the Trinity is described. The fact that the Father is eternal (is, was, is to come) shows that God will be there to fulfill His promises. He is able to do all He has promised.

The Spirit (v. 4c). Next John describes the Holy Spirit who is before the throne of God. The phrase "seven spirits" does not mean there are seven different Holy Spirits. Rather, this is a way of referring to the Holy Spirit before the throne. The writer alludes to the seven biblical characteristics of the Holy Spirit (Isa. 11:2; cf. Rev. 4:5).

The Son (vv. 5-8). The Book of Revelation emphasizes Jesus Christ, the coming Judge and King of the earth. How can He be described? John uses three titles which show Jesus' past, present, and future. He is the "Faithful Witness," the One who came to reveal God in His life on the earth. He is the "First-born of the dead," the first to be raised never to die again. This is why He can be in heaven helping and comforting us today. He is also the "Ruler of the kings of the earth," the One who will come to rule this world with a rod of iron.

What has Christ done for you and me? First, He has loved us (v. 5) and has shown that love by dying for us. Second, He has released us from our sins (v. 5), which means our salvation is dependent on Him and Him alone. This was accomplished by His blood, that is His death, which alone paid the penalty for our sins. Third, He has made us a kingdom (v. 6), not a kingdom of citizens or soldiers, but a kingdom of priests. This gives us the important responsibilities of worshipping and honoring Him. We who have nothing and were nothing have received everything by His grace. This is why the writer includes a doxology to Him (v. 6); for to Him and Him alone is glory and dominion forever.

Many ask the question: "When will Christ return?" The writer points to that great day when He will come to this earth to rule (v. 7). He will come from heaven in the clouds. He will be visible to all, for every eye will see Him. His coming will be accompanied by mourning; for while some will cry for joy, others will weep because of coming judgment. Not only this verse, but also the rest of Revelation is about the coming of Jesus Christ, and in the succeeding chapters John will describe how Christ's coming will take place.

Like the Father, the Son is also eternal and will fulfill all He has promised (v. 8). This is why the Greek letters *alpha* and *omega* are used, the first and last letters of the Greek alphabet. Jesus Christ is the first and last, the beginning and ending of all things. He will be faithful to His word. His coming is assured.

The Picture [1:9-18]

Where John was (1:9-10). John was on the island of Patmos, a small island off the southwestern coast of modern Turkey. He was there because of the word of God and his own testimony to Jesus. That is, because he had been faithful in proclaiming God's message, he was exiled to that island. From Patmos, John wrote to the churches in the Roman province of Asia Minor.

The Book of Revelation is a record of what John saw and heard from the Lord. This is the meaning of the phrase "in the Spirit" (v. 10). This vision occurred on the Lord's Day, Sunday, the day of the week when Christians especially remembered the Lord.

What John heard (vv. 10-11). John heard the sound of a voice that came to him sharply like a trumpet. This voice commanded him to write what he saw in a book and send it to the seven churches. So John was God's messenger to give the message to the churches, and to us.

What John saw (vv. 12-16). When John heard the voice, he naturally turned to see who had spoken. What he saw was a most unusual scene, and one he describes carefully for us.

John first saw seven golden lampstands (v. 12). He didn't see a seven pronged lampstand as described in the Old Testament, but rather seven separate lampstands. They were probably arranged in a circle with the Son of Man standing in the middle of them. The lampstands represented the seven churches (v. 20). Christ was in the middle for He was the One the Church should reflect.

Next, John described Christ dressed as He one day will be when He comes to judge the world. Christ wore a robe that reached to His feet. He had a golden girdle, which showed His deity. His white hair emphasized His authority, for He was older and wiser than others. His eyes were like a flame of fire, penetrating, showing discernment and omniscience. His feet were like burnished bronze, the metal of which the altar, the place of judgment in the Old Testament, was made. His voice was like the sound of many waters, showing His universality and authority.

What did Christ hold in His right hand, the place of privilege? As John looked he saw seven stars, the angels or messengers of the churches (v. 16; cf. v. 20). Doesn't the messenger of the Church today also need to be in the hand of Christ? Only then can he have God's message, and only then can it be delivered with authority to the people. The messenger also has the responsibility of staying in God's hand.

From Christ's mouth came a sharp two-edged sword, the symbol of the Word of God, which penetrates not only one's actions but also one's motives (Heb. 4:12). When Christ judges, He will judge the hearts of all people. John also saw Christ's face shining like the sun, showing John the beauty of His Person.

What John did (vv. 17-18). What did John do when he saw Christ? He fell at His feet as a dead man, for he was afraid (v. 17). But the Lord said, "Do not be afraid." Since He is the Source of all things, He has a purpose in the coming judgment. He is also the One with the keys of death and Hades. One day the graves will be opened and some will rise first to reign with Him. Later, others will rise to be judged by Him. But it is Christ who has the keys.

The Church today needs a fresh vision of Christ, as did the Apostle John. We should not fear Christ, but realize He is the One who is sufficient for any task today. We tend to focus our eyes on other people rather than on our Saviour. But when we see Christ as John saw Him, then we can see what He is able to do. As the Gospels show us what Christ did while here on the earth, the Book of Revelation shows us what He will do in the future. As we look at both, we will be helped in our service for Him today.

The Positions

Preterist. How should we interpret the events of this book? There are various positions of interpretation regarding John's vision. For instance, there is the preterist view which holds that these events have already been fulfilled in the early history of the church. The word *preterist* is from the Latin word which means "past." According to this interpretation, John described the church's victory over Judaism in chapters 5—11; he recorded the victory over Rome in chapters 12—19; and he saw the glory of those victories in chapters 20—22. The persecutions described were those which occurred at the time of the Roman Empire.

Historical. This viewpoint holds that the Book of Revelation gives a panorama of the history of the church from the time of John to the end of the age. The many symbols speak of the papacy and the corruption and wars of the church throughout history. The book is therefore in the process of being fulfilled throughout the whole Christian era. Many of the reformers held to this interpretive view.

Idealist. Some believe that the Book of Revelation is only a series of symbols which represent the struggle between good and evil. The book is therefore spiritualized and the details are unimportant and do not need to be "fulfilled." Its message is only that God one day will be victorious over evil.

Futurist. There are those, however, who believe in a literal interpretation and expect that most of the events recorded in this book will occur in the future. The events from chapter 4 onward are yet to be fulfilled, for nothing in history adequately fulfills these passages. No judgments have ever equalled those recorded in chapters 6, 8—9, and 16. There have never been any resurrections like those recorded in chapter 20. Christ has not yet returned visibly as described in chapter 19.

The Purpose [1:19-20]

Which of these positions are correct? Verse 19 helps us to understand. Here God commands John to write three things: the things which he has seen—past tense; the things which are—present tense; and the things which shall take place after these things—future tense. Since John was obedient to God's command, this is a God-inspired outline for the book. As such, we will find these three major divisions in the Book of Revelation.

Since John receives this command at the end of chapter 1, the first section must be chapter 1, the things which he has seen—that is, his vision of Christ. The second section is the things which are, the messages to the seven churches recorded in chapters 2 and 3. The third section, the future section, begins with chapter 4 and continues to the end of the book (4:1 uses the same wording, in the Greek text, as 1:19). For this reason, we will use the futurist interpretive view in this book.

Chapter one is a fitting introduction to a book which declares that Christ one day will return to set up His kingdom on the earth. We may be surrounded by many problems, but one day Christ will return to set *everything* right.

We do not have to wait until Christ returns, however, to be living for Him and serving Him. We need to realize where this world is headed and gear our lives in light of Christ's imminent return. This is why John wrote elsewhere in the Bible, "And every man that hath this hope in Him, purifieth himself, even as He is pure" (1 John 3:3). The study of the Book of Revelation should have an effect on our day-by-day living. Perhaps this is why God promises a special blessing for those who read, hear, and heed the words of Revelation (Rev. 1:3).

2
God
Solves
Our
Problems
(Revelation 2)

Have you ever faced any of these situations?

"I don't know if I can commit myself to lead a Junior Sunday School Class," Bob confided. "I used to be so excited about the church and service there, but now I've lost interest. Oh, I still go, but I can't get involved enthusiastically."

The sight was pathetic and the words seemed desperate. "I don't know why I'm here," the shriveled little lady told me from her bed. "Of all the diseases I know of, I never would have asked for cancer. I hope I learn what this is all about, for I am sure miserable."

"Our church really used to be on fire for God," the church leader said. "But we're in a community that doesn't appreciate us. Rather than competing with all that's happening, we let all the groups use our building. Oh, we still try to have a meeting once a week, but it's hard to tell the difference between our church and the community."

All of us face problems. For some there are the problems of pressure and spiritual drift, growing cold to the things of God. For others there are the problems of pain and suffering. For still others there are the problems of being surrounded and taken in by the world to which we minister.

These problems are similar to those the early church faced centuries ago. Community values rubbed off on early Christians and many were taken in by them. Whole churches suffered because they were engulfed by their city culture. Many became so side-tracked that they lost their effectiveness for God. But basic solutions to these problems were clearly laid out for them, solutions we still need to follow today.

What kinds of churches were established in the first century? Although many first-century churches existed, seven are of particular significance. John wrote to these congregation members and gave them special instructions for their problems. Those of us who have similar problems should follow these instructions, too. As God solved their problems then, He can solve ours now.

Each of these seven churches was located in a city of Asia Minor, the area east of Greece in what is modern-day Turkey. These strategic cities formed a circle with roads connecting them. The messages Christ gave are arranged in order by the geographical location of the cities—beginning with the largest city (Ephesus) and going in a clockwise direction to the other cities.

Many of us have one or more of the crucial problems that Christ mentioned in these seven church letters of Revelation 2—3. But Jesus, as the Builder of the church, can solve the problems we face. He is looking for people to do what He commands and to trust in His solutions to their spiritual needs. It is important not only to examine the details of each of these letters, but also to put into practice the instructions Jesus gives. These letters from the Lord have a lot of practical application for us. The content of each letter can be outlined under five major points: the church, Christ, the commendation, the consideration, and the commitment. Let's take a look at the first four letters, found in Revelation 2.

The Letter to Ephesus [2:1-7]

The church (2:1). The city of Ephesus was the largest of the seven cities and the capital of the Roman province of Asia. Known as "the first and greatest metropolis of Asia," it was important for three reasons. First, the city of Ephesus was a crucial commercial and political center. It was located at the mouth of the Cayster river, and important trade routes of the world ran through it. It was a city of approximately 300,000 people with an amphitheater that could hold about 25,000 people. At the time of the early church, the city had been in existence for over 1,000 years.

Another reason for its importance was the temple of Artemis (Latin, meaning "Diana"), one of the seven wonders of the world. The huge temple measured about 340 by 164 feet, for it honored an important Greek goddess. When sailors from the Aegean Sea looked at it from a distance and saw the temple still standing, they felt secure.

A third reason for this city's importance was the church situated there. Paul established the Ephesian church on his third missionary journey (Acts 19) and it was a center for the spreading of the Gospel. Timothy later ministered there, as did the Apostle John. John wrote four books of the New Testament from Ephesus.

Who is the angel mentioned in verse 1? Some believe churches, like nations, have angels assigned to them. For instance, Michael is assigned to Israel and another is assigned to Persia (Dan. 12:1; 10:13). But the word "angel" may also be translated "messenger" and is used to refer to human beings (Luke 9:52; James 2:25). As such, "angel" refers to the leader of the Ephesian church.

Christ (v. 1). How is Christ pictured as He speaks to this church? The Apostle John sees Him holding the stars walking in the midst of the lampstands. The stars represent the messengers of the seven churches (1:20). Christ holds the stars in His right hand, the position of authority. This is as it should be, for the leaders of the church should receive their authority from the Lord. Sometimes they may try to crawl out from that position; and when they do, they sink like Peter, who took his eyes off the Lord.

That Christ is walking in the midst of the lampstands, identified as the churches (1:20), shows His active concern for them. The golden lampstands signify the importance of the church to the Lord. The church is to be the witness for Christ in the world. It is His inheritance, which He purchased with His own blood (Acts 20:28). Although the church is not perfect, Christ is preparing it for its place in heaven. He therefore sees the church as golden.

The commendation (v. 2-3). Christ encourages the Ephesian church before He speaks of its problem. The believers at Thessalonica had been commended for their "work of faith and labor of love and steadfastness of hope" (1 Thes. 1:3, NASB). Is it therefore possible to have only activity without purpose, only work without any real goal? Many today are in this same situation.

Christ also commended this church for its loyalty. They had not compromised with false teachers. They had heeded the warning that Satan's messengers could be dressed up as angels of light (2 Cor. 11:13). There can be false teachers in any church. But the church at Ephesus had not tolerated them; the Ephesian believers had tested them and found them to be untrue.

These people were also commended for their endurance in the cause of Christ. Many believers become impatient with the work of God. When they do not receive immediate or visible answers, they believe God is not working. But God is not deaf, nor is He dead—He is accomplishing His purposes. This is the advantage of being older in the Lord, for one can look back and see what God has done in the lives of others. This church persevered.

The consideration (vv. 4-6). With such a word of commendation, what was this church's problem? The congregation had left its first love (v. 4). Its love for the Lord had grown cold and stagnant.

Love is an emotion which, if not stimulated, will fade. It needs to be cultivated in order to keep its vitality and vibrancy. This church had not cultivated its love for the Lord and, as a result, that love had grown cold. They were drifting away from the Lord.

The writer to the Hebrews warned his readers about drifting away from the Word of God (Heb. 2:1). The word *drift* was a term used of ships drifting out to sea. As ships slowly drift away from the harbor, so believers can drift away from God. This is why our love for God needs constantly to be rekindled if we are to accomplish God's purposes in our lives.

How can this lack of love be remedied? The answer is given in the three "Rs" of verse 5. First, they were to *remember* from where they had fallen. They had to go back to where they had left the Lord and remember Him that they might love Him. Second, they were to *repent* and do the deeds they had done at first. The word "repent" means to change one's mind, so they were to change their minds about the Lord. They were to do the things they had done for Him at the beginning, when their love was blazing hot. Third, if they did not do this, God would *remove* their lampstand out of its place. They would lose their opportunity to serve God, and the lampstand that once burned brightly would no longer be a witness for the Lord.

What did they do? It would have been wonderful if they had obeyed the Lord and returned to Him. But there is no lampstand in Ephesus today—the city is a site for archeological study. God has removed that lampstand out of its place of service. To God, our faithful service is important (1 Cor. 4:2). Those who are faithful in His service will be rewarded. This was the message to the church at Ephesus, and it is a message to us as well.

The problem of the church at Ephesus did not diminish its contempt for the deeds of the Nicolaitans (v. 6). Who were these people? They could have been followers of Nicolas, an early church leader (Acts 6:5), who some say later led a group that promoted looseness in Christian conduct. Or they could have been a group (the name means *conquering of the people*) that promoted a clerical hierarchy. Either way, we should find out which things displease God so we will not do them.

The commitment (v. 7). Although this message was especially given to the church at Ephesus, all believers are to obey this instruction. It is for one to hear "that hath an ear" (v. 7). Believers will enjoy the tree of life, the promise of eternal life, which Adam lost when he sinned against God. What a blessing it is to have a right relationship with God and to live for Him!

The Letter to Smyrna [2:8-11]

The church (2:8). About 35 miles from Ephesus was the city of Smyrna on the site of modern Izmir, Turkey. The beautiful city curved around the bay of Smyrna at the base of Mount Pagous. With a population of about 200,000, the city had temples, public buildings, and a library. The city planners laid out everything to enhance the city's beauty, including the streets, one which was known as "the street of gold."

The name Smyrna comes from the same linguistic root as the word *myrrh*. Myrrh was a perfume substance, like a piece of chalk, which had to be broken to emit its fragrance. For this reason, myrrh spoke of suffering and death, and is used three times in the Gospels concerning the death of Christ. As a gift brought by the wisemen (Matt. 2:11), myrrh pointed toward Christ's death. And it was actually used to embalm Christ's body after His death (Mark 15:23; John 19:39). The church of Smyrna is known as the suffering church.

Christ (v. 8). How is Christ pictured as He addresses this church? He is the First and Last, the Eternal One who is the source of all things including life itself. Moreover, He is the One who was once dead and has come back to life. Can He not therefore give comfort to us in time of suffering and answer the problem of death itself?

The commendation (v. 9). This important church was commended for three reasons. First, it was commended because of its tribulation and affliction. Suffering is real and difficult, though only for this life. Second, it was commended for its poverty, a poverty that was outward not inward. One may give the appearance of poverty on the outside, but, as with this church, be rich spiritually. The believers at Smyrna knew the Lord and were living for Him, in sharp contrast to the believers at Laodicea (cf. 3:17). Third, the church at Smyrna was commended because it was blasphemed by the Judaizers. Those were legalists who believed in keeping the Mosaic Law rather than receiving the grace of God. They were servants not of God but of Satan, people who were trying to substitute something else for God's grace.

The consideration (v. 10). What will happen to these people? Does God promise they will be removed from the place of suffering? Not at all. Rather, they are promised the presence of God during this dreadful time. God does not promise to remove us from the sphere of testing, but He does promise to be with us in the midst of such trials.

What caused this church to suffer? Perhaps the Judaizers were persecuting these people. Or perhaps the Roman Empire was hurting this church. Although we do not know the exact reason, their suffering was real.

Why do Christians suffer today? Some suffering may be because of sin, for God promises to discipline His children (Heb. 12:6). Not all suffering is a result of sin, however, but suffering is a result of God's sovereign purpose. For instance, Job suffered not because of sin, but to bring glory to the Lord through his suffering. Paul suffered not because of sin, but because his thorn in the flesh was a messenger from Satan. The same may be true of many of us today. But, as with Job and Paul, so it is with us; God's grace is sufficient in suffering and His power is perfected in weakness (2 Cor. 12:9).

How long are we to endure suffering? The church at Smyrna

endured suffering for a short time, 10 days. For us also, suffering is for a brief time, since it is only encountered in this life. We are therefore to be faithful, even unto death, for all things are in God's control and He is going to give us the crown of life (v. 10). The word *crown* means a victor's crown and the faithful ones will be victorious in the midst of suffering.

The commitment (v. 11). The one who overcomes will not be hurt by the second death. This death involves being eternally separated from God in the lake of fire (Rev. 20:11-15). Although there may be some suffering now, the prospect of the future is bright and glorious.

The Letter to Pergamum [2:12-17]

The church (2:12). The next city in clockwise order was Pergamum, a beautiful city laid out on hillside terraces above the fertile valley of the Caicus River. It was known for its art and sculpture, including a sculpted altar of Zeus which some thought was Satan's throne (2:13). The city had a large library, and this may have been where scholars first used parchment.

Christ (v. 12). Here John pictures Christ as the One who has the sharp two-edged sword. He is able to give penetrating judgment, piercing our work and the motive behind that work. A place like Satan's throne will need such judgment.

The commendation (v. 13). What really was Satan's throne? It could have been the Roman god Zeus, or perhaps the Roman emperor, or even the city's whole religious system of worshiping pagan gods. In spite of such surroundings, the church there did not deny their faith in God. A good example of such faith was Antipas, who was martyred for the cause of Christ. Do we have such faith as this today?

The consideration (vv. 14-16). Even those with such faith, however, can have problems. There were those within the church who held to the teachings of Balaam and others who held to the teachings of the Nicolaitans. False teachers in the church caused the problem.

Who was Balaam? He was the one who taught Balak to put a stumbling block before Israel by eating things sacrificed to idols and commiting acts of immorality (Num. 22—25). All those who do religious works for personal gain are like Balaam. Whereas the church at Ephesus condemned the Nicolaitans (cf. 2:6), the church at Pergamum tolerated them.

The problem with the believers at Pergamum was that instead of the believers transforming society, society was transforming them. They were being squeezed into the mold of this world, rather than being pilgrims on the earth and witnesses for Jesus Christ.

What was the remedy for such a serious problem? Repentance (v. 16). These people were to change their minds about what they were doing and get back to the way of the Lord. If not, there would be immediate judgment and the Lord would remove their opportunity for service. Did He not do this with Demas (2 Tim. 4:10), and could He not do this with us?

The commitment (v. 17). For all those who overcome, God promises three special blessings. First, they will be given the hidden manna. As the Israelites were given manna each day to sustain themselves, so the believer is given Christ, the hidden manna, to sustain himself in the midst of his problems. Second, they will be given a white stone. This refers to the ancient custom of voting for an accused person and acquitting that person by casting a white stone. The believer has been acquitted of his sin by believing in Christ as his Saviour (cf. Rom. 8:1). Third, they will be given a new name which no one knows, a name that will show the very presence of Christ. The believer has the sufficiency of Christ, acquittal from the judgment of sin, and the very presence of Christ dwelling in his life. With this fortification, he can be victorious over the world in which he lives. But the key is the living power of Christ.

The Letter to Thyatira [2:18-29]

The church (2:18). The city of Thyatira was an important trading city, located 52 miles northeast of Smyrna. Lydia, the seller of purple fabrics and first convert in the church of Philippi (Acts 16:14), was from Thyatira. The city may have been evangelized from the church at Ephesus (cf. Acts 19:10).

Christ (v. 18). Because of what was happening in this church, Christ is seen as the coming Judge. Eyes as a flame of fire show His omniscience, and feet like fine brass refer to the brass altar of the Old Testament, the place of judgment. Christ one day will judge perfectly and righteously.

The commendation (v. 19). This church is commended for its love, faith, service, perseverance, but especially for its works. The church was known for its activity, but not for its fruit. There is a big difference between doing a lot of activity on the one hand and accomplishing God's purpose on the other.

The consideration (vv. 20-25). The problem with this church was that it tolerated open apostasy and idolatry. Within it there was a Jezebel, possibly the real name of the woman, or one who behaved like the Jezebel of the Old Testament (1 Kings 16:31-32). What did this woman do? She led God's servants astray. When she was asked to repent she refused. The result will be God's judgment. He will "kill her children," the churches will know who He is, and He will reward believers according to their deeds (v. 23).

Notice that this false teaching is called "the depths of Satan" (v. 24). As Satan had a synagogue in Smyrna (v. 9), and a throne in Pergamum (v. 13), he also has "deep things" of false doctrine *in the church* of Thyatira (v. 24).

What was the remedy for this? First, that judgment has to come because of the sin involved (v. 23). But the church is told to take what it has and "hold fast till I come" (v. 25). Believers are to cling to the things of God until Christ's return.

The commitment (vv. 26-29). Those who overcome are given

authority over the nations. One day Christ Himself will rule the nations with a rod of iron. They are also given the Morning Star, a reference to the presence of Christ Himself. Believers have the power and presence of Christ in their lives.

Which of these churches' problems do we face today? What is the major problem in your life? Is it drifting away from your love for the Lord; is it suffering; is it dwelling in the world; or is it open apostasy and idolatry? In each case, God gives His remedy, and we need to follow it. Only in this way can we please God.

3
What Prophecy Is Fulfilled Today?

(Revelation 3)

The long, black limousines rolled up to the impressive concrete and steel hotel. Men carrying briefcases and dressed in black and gray business suits stepped quickly through the hotel lobby and went directly to the Grand Ballroom. Each picked up pen and notepaper to jot down important words and phrases as he listened intently to the speaker.

This was a seminar for the major businessmen of the world. Each had prepared carefully for the meeting. Each had jetted in directly from his place of business. And each had paid a large fee for what he considered to be the most important economic meeting of the year.

During the course of the next three days, these business people would hear speakers talking about interest rates, inflation, and the money markets of the world. Each authority would give his views about what would happen in the next year. And each speaker would be partially right, but in many cases wrong.

Business seminars, economic meetings, and marketing sessions are held almost daily throughout the world. In each of these meetings, many predictions are made regarding the future. But all such predictions contain a great amount of uncertainty or risk.

However, what God says about the future is in sharp contrast to all of this. There is no uncertainty or inaccuracy. Promises of the future can be checked against predicted happenings of the past. Much has already been carefully and minutely fulfilled.

Consider, for example, some major fulfilled prophecies. The city of Tyre was swept as clean as a bare rock by Alexander the Great, just as the Prophet Ezekiel had declared it would be (Ezek. 26:3-14). World empires came and went exactly as the Prophet Daniel foretold (Dan. 2; 7). Jesus Christ was born in Bethlehem, lived on the earth, died on a cross, and rose from the dead on the third day precisely as the Old Testament had predicted (Micah 5:2; Isa. 61:1-2; Ps. 22; Ps. 16:10). Since so many prophecies were accurately fulfilled in the past, it seems reasonable to expect the other prophecies to be fulfilled in the future.

The Book of Revelation foretells the future. It speaks of events that will take place on the earth before Christ comes to set up His kingdom. One day all will be fulfilled just as John predicted.

If the Bible records prophecies of the past and of the future, one question many ask is, "What about today? Are there any prophecies that will be fulfilled during this age?"

Jesus spoke of many things that would happen during this age. He spoke of the coming of the Holy Spirit, the founding and growth of the church, and the responsibility of carrying the Gospel to the ends of the earth. But in two special passages, He gave the pattern and program of the present age, an outline of what is happening today.

One of those passages is in Matthew 13, where Jesus gives seven parables that show what will happen on earth before He comes to set up His kingdom. The parables of the sower and the seed, the wheat and the tares, the treasure, the pearl of great price, etc. fit in here.

The other passage is in Revelation 2—3, the letters to the seven churches. As we have seen, each of these letters was written to a real first-century church, a *particular assembly*. In addition, since all Scripture is profitable, each of these letters is profitable for us; each has important *practical application*. But we should notice something else. If we were to take a sheet of paper and in one column list in order the seven churches, and in another make an outline of the major stages of the history of the church, we would see an interesting correlation. These churches, in order, form an outline of the *present age*. Together, they form seven eras or periods of time that prophesy the course of the age until Christ returns to the earth. Could this be what Christ meant when He told John to write "the things which *are*"? (1:19)

Viewed in this way, what do these letters depict? The church of Ephesus illustrates the church at the close of the apostolic age, when it was drifting away from its love for the Lord. The church of Smyrna pictures the time of the great persecutions (A.D. 100-312) when the church suffered greatly for the cause of Christ. The church of Pergamum, whose name means "marriage," illustrates the church married to the world when Constantine united church and state (A.D. 313-500). The church of Thyatira illustrates the Roman church in the Middle Ages (A.D. 500-1500). Assuming this is true, the following three churches are of particular significance.

The Letter to Sardis (3:1-6)

The church (3:1). Located about 50 miles east of Smyrna and 30 miles south of Thyatira, the city of Sardis was the capital of the Roman province of Lydia. The major trade routes between the Aegean Sea and the inland provinces of Asia and Galatia went through Sardis.

During the time of the early church, Sardis was a wealthy and prosperous city. It had a huge temple to the Greek goddess Artemis and a large Jewish synagogue. The name *Sardis* is from a Hebrew word meaning "those who have escaped," or "remnant." The period of time illustrated by the church of Sardis was the Reformation, a time when many churches were marked by outward ritualism and inward deadness. This was the problem of the church of Sardis.

Christ (v. 1). Christ is pictured as the One who has the seven Spirits of God, showing His wisdom, and the seven stars or messengers of the churches (cf. 1:20). He is the One who controls the leadership of the church, if they will let Him. In this case, the leadership had allowed the church to deteriorate.

The commendation (v. 1). God gives one point of commendation to this church, its name. Although the church seemed to be dead, it had a name which meant "remnant," and *some* people in the church were spiritually alive.

In spite of problems with the church, God always has a remnant. This was true during the time of Elijah, when he wondered if he were the only one who had not bowed his knee to Baal (1 Kings 19:10-18). This was true in the time of the Apostle Paul, when there were those who thought God had forsaken His nation, Israel (Rom. 11). And it had also been true down through the history of the church. Believers may sometimes be in the minority, but with God they always are in the majority.

The consideration (vv. 1-4). What was wrong with this church? God indicted the Sardis church in four ways. First, some members in this church were spiritually dead (v. 1). The name Sardis may mean "remnant," but their works showed a definite lack of spiritual life.

Second, other members in this church were ready to give up spiritually (v. 2). Not only were some members spiritually dead, but others also were falling apart inside. They needed to give full attention to the problem at hand. They needed to wake up and strengthen the things that remained.

Third, their works were not fulfilled or completed before God

(v. 2). People may be very active in the church, but unless this activity is produced by the Spirit of God, nothing is really accomplished. Jesus said, "Apart from Me you can do nothing" (John 15:5, NIV).

Fourth, some members in this church were defiled (v. 4). A few had not soiled their garments, but many had. They were in no way serving the Lord. What was the solution? The message was clear: (1) remember, (2) hold fast, and (3) repent (v. 3). They were to change their minds and get moving in the Chistian faith. Otherwise, God would come for them in judgment.

The commitment (vv. 4-6). For those who were overcoming, who had not soiled their garments, what were they promised? First, they would walk with Christ in white. They would be rewarded for their faithfulness, for being true to the Lord. Second, their names would not be blotted out of the Book of Life. They would be certain of their salvation (a double negative is used in the original text). Third, they would be confessed before the Father and the angels. Here is strong assurance from the Lord concerning His people.

The Letter to Philadelphia [3:7-13]

The church (3:7). The city of Philadelphia was located 26 miles east of Sardis on a high hill overlooking a major Roman road that led to the interior of modern Turkey. A commercial center, Philadelphia became very prosperous. Many people lived outside the city proper because it was subject to earthquakes. Tiberius reconstructed the city after a devastating earthquake, and it was to the church in this reconstructed city that John wrote.

The name of the city means "brotherly love," and the name pictures the great missionary vision and expansion of the church during the last two centuries.

Christ (v. 7). How is Christ pictured as He addresses this important church? First, His character is emphasized. He is holy and true, the One from whom all evil is absent and the One who conforms to reality. Since this is true of Christ, should it not also be true of His followers?

Second, His authority is noted. He has the key of David, that is, He is sovereign and able to carry out His purposes. Third, His activity is mentioned; He is the One who is able to open and permanently shut doors. This authority and activity was illustrated by God's servant Eliakim in the Old Testament (cf. Isa. 22:22).

The commendation (v. 8). Everything was right in the Philadelphia church, certainly an illustration of God's true church. There are four marks of commendation. First, their opportunity. They had before them an open door of service which no one could shut. Second, their power. They were able to accomplish what God directed. Third, their stability. They had studied and kept His Word. Fourth, their testimony. They had not apostatized; they had not denied His name.

The commitment (3:9-13). The church at Philadelphia was a most unusual church in that nothing evil was recorded. The Lord does not point out any specific problem in this church. It is a church that lives for and serves the Lord. As a result, Christ gives a special message to this church of what He will do for them.

First, there is a commitment to defeat their enemies (v. 9). What enemies did these people face? They were known as Judaizers, a group that plagued the early church. Judaizers wanted people to keep the Mosaic Law not only for salvation but also for Christian living. The Jerusalem Council declared that the Law of Moses was not necessary for salvation (Acts 15). And Paul declared that the Law was not necessary for sanctification (Rom. 7). But this group wanted to get back to the Law of Moses and constantly stirred up the people. God declared that He would take care of this opposition; He would give this church victory over their enemies. One day their enemies would bow at their feet.

There are lessons here for us. The Lord will judge our enemies

(Rom. 12:19), and we should *leave* the judging to Him. Also, one day all, including our enemies, will bow before Him (Phil. 2:10). How much better to recognize Him as our Saviour now rather than as our Judge then!

Second, there is a commitment to deliver from tribulation (vv. 10-11). God promises to keep the church from the time of testing that is to come.

Previously, the Lord had told His followers that they would endure tribulation, persecution, and affliction in the world (John 16:33). But a special time of testing is coming, a special hour of tribulation, upon the whole earth. Different from the normal perse-cution believers suffer today, this is a time which will have as its purpose judgment on those who "dwell on the earth," those whose lives are wrapped up in the things of earth. (This concept is used throughout Revelation to describe unbelievers, cf. 6:10; 8:13; 11:1; 12:12; 13:8, 12, 14; 17:2, 8.)

What is the promise to believers? They will be kept from this time of tribulation's very hour. God will remove them first before this time of tribulation comes on the earth, and He judges unbe-lievers.

In light of this, we have the promise that Christ will come quickly (v. 11). This same promise is repeated in the last chapter of this book (22:7, 12, 20). The hope of the believer is not in the Tribulation, or even in the signs of the end of the age. Rather, the hope of the believer is in the Saviour from heaven who will one day come for him (cf. 1 Thes. 1:10). What should believers do in the meantime? They should hold fast to what they have. They should keep on keeping on. They should continue trusting the Lord to fulfill all He has promised and live today in the light of eternity.

Third, there is a commitment to honor the believers throughout eternity (vv. 12-13). As dignitaries in the city of Philadelphia had pillars erected to them, so believers will be pillars in the temple of God. They will have a strategic place throughout eternity.

The believer also will have three names. He will have the name of "My God." This name emphasizes God's "ownership" of the believer. He will also have the name of the "city of My God." This emphasizes his citizenship in the heavenly city, the New Jerusalem. Then too he will have written on him "My new name." This emphasizes his universal role before God. What a prospect for believers in this church and for all who know Christ as Saviour!

The Letter to Laodicea [3:14-22]

The church (3:14). Located in the interior of modern Turkey, 10 miles from the city of Colosse, this final city was important for several reasons. First, it was known for its lukewarm water. The water came from hot springs some distance away and was piped through blocks of stone. But by the time the water reached the city, it was neither hot enough for the public baths nor cold enough to drink.

Second, it was known for its wealth, because of its commercial location and its banking interests. The people were so wealthy that once, after an earthquake destroyed the city, they rebuilt the city out of their own funds.

Third, it was known for its black wool. This was an especially fine quality wool, and the garments made from it were in great demand.

Fourth, it was known for its eye powder. This was a special salve used in the treatment of eye diseases and known as the powder from Phrygia, the Roman province near where this city was located. We will see that all of Laodicea's physical characteristics are spiritually applied in this letter to the church, representing the highly organized, but unbelieving church which will be on earth at the end of the age.

Christ (3:14). How is Christ pictured as He addresses this church? He is seen in three ways. First, He is the Amen, the One who has final authority over all things, including the judgment of this church. Second, He is the faithful and true Witness. He is the One who sees all things and testifies accurately of them. God cannot look in an approving manner on sin, but that does not mean sin is hidden from God. God is omniscient. He knows and sees all things and gives an account of His witness. Third, He is the Beginning, or, better rendered, Chief of the creation of God. Christ has priority over all of God's creation for He is before all, has created all, and in Him all consist (Col. 1:15-17). As such, He is the standard by which all of God's creation must be measured. This includes the church of Laodicea.

The condemnation (3:15-17). This church is condemned for two major reasons. First, it is condemned because of its works, which were neither cold nor hot (vv. 15-16). In other words, there was nothing of value there. The believers were lukewarm like their own water supply. And since such works indicated one's faith, their works demonstrated there was no faith. This is why God promises to spit (literally, vomit) them out of His mouth.

The other reason for their condemnation is that they had external wealth but internal poverty (v. 17). They had material blessings but spiritual misery. From their perspective they had everything, but from God's perspective they had nothing. On the outside material things satisfied them, but inside they were empty. How can one "buy" inner joy or peace? How can one get rid of guilt?

This local church was made up of only Christians who went through the motions, but who were not really saved. Men must have a need before God can fill it; they must recognize their emptiness. But these people were satisfied with themselves and with their external substitutes for God. They did not want to be saved because they did not feel lost! They went to church, sang the songs, but never entered into a personal relationship with God. They were imitators, not participators. There are some in our churches today who fit into this same category.

The commitment (vv. 18-22). Because of this church's dire

need, Christ says nothing good about it at all. He gives only condemnation. But He does counsel them as to what they *should* do.

What does this church need? First, the church needs God's gold, not theirs (v. 18). Their gold was temporary; the value would change; it could rust and corrupt. God's "gold," His instruction, would show the fact of sin and their need for a Saviour. God's Word was even better than gold (Ps. 19:10-11) and they should follow its teachings.

Second, the church of Laodicea needed His clothing, not theirs. Clothing, in Scripture, is a picture of the righteousness of God, that which He alone can give. Their righteousness was like filthy rags (Isa. 64:6). When one accepts Christ as Saviour, he is given the righteousness of God (Rom. 3:22; 5:17). He is clothed with white raiment.

Third, they needed His eyesalve, not theirs. Instead of having their eyes anointed with the Phrygian eye powder, they needed the eye powder that comes from God. This was a reference to the Holy Spirit who alone can open people's eyes. They needed to be zealous and repent, or to change their minds (v. 19). They needed to accept Christ as Saviour and He would give them inner satisfaction.

Where is Christ in relationship to this church? He is on the outside, knocking to get in (v. 20). Christ wants these people, and all people who do not know Him as Saviour, to open their lives to Him. When they do, He will come into their lives and have fellowship with them. Salvation means not only being delivered from the penalty of sin, but also being brought into fellowship with God through Jesus Christ.

What is promised to those who overcome? They will reign with the Lord in His coming kingdom (v. 21). When Jesus Christ finished His work of redemption, He sat down at the right hand of the throne of God (Heb. 1:3). But one day, when He comes again,

He will be seated on His own throne. Believers will be seated with Him as they reign with Him during that time. This reign is described in the last chapters of this book.

These then were the seven churches and the messages Christ gave to them. They were particular assemblies to which these letters were written. From these letters, we find much practical application for our lives. But these seven letters also may indicate the course of this present age. If so, we may be approaching the Laodicean church age, a time of the professing church. This age will live up to the meaning of the name Laodicea, "the judgment of the people."

If we are approaching this Laodicean age, we will enjoy vast opportunities of service. Never before will there be such a need for the message of the Word of God. It is therefore imperative for us to study what God says and to share it with others.

But it will also be a time of spiritual confusion when it will be difficult to tell who really is and who is not a Christian. This is because those in the world sometimes look very good and believers sometimes look bad. Jesus said that the "wheat" and "tares" would grow together in this age. We therefore need to be visible demonstrations of the life He gives. We need to be living day by day for the Lord in order that we may be good examples before others.

4
What
Is
Heaven
Like?

(Revelation 4—5)

The appointment was for one hour, but it had taken weeks to prepare for it. The itinerary had been carefully planned, special clothes purchased, a culture tutor hired. "I am so excited," the wife said. "I can't believe we've been invited."

Days before the event, the couple arrived at their hotel. They familiarized themselves with the route to the palace and rehearsed the fine points of etiquette. They reviewed every movement they would make and tried to gauge the reaction. Finally, the big day arrived.

Both rose early and went over the day's activities. They dressed on schedule and were picked up in their special limousine. "I must see your invitation," the guard at the entry house said. After he checked both the invitation and the couple, they proceeded to the impressive entryway, where the doorman helped them out of the car. Then, they went into the palace waiting room.

"This is a very special time in our lives," the man confided to his wife. "It will always be an evening to remember."

At the exact announced moment, they were escorted down the

palace hallway, through the huge doors, and into a very large room. The windows were lavishly decorated, and masterpiece paintings hung on the walls. Even the ceiling was made of special wood gathered from various countries. Velvet-dressed court attendants formed a human corridor up to the throne. Finally, after being properly announced, the university president and his wife met the king.

Being in the presence of a human king, however, is nothing compared to being in the presence of the sovereign King of the universe. One day we will enter heaven and be taken to the very throne room of God. There will be able to praise Him and glorify Him visibly and personally as we stand in His presence.

The Apostle John, by means of a vision, was taken into the very presence of God the King. There he described the throne room in all its beauty and splendor. He also portrayed the beings that will stand in God's presence, and recorded the praise and adoration given the King of kings.

Chapter 4 of Revelation begins the third and final division of this book as outlined in Revelation 1:19. God told John to write the things which he had seen (chap. 1), the things which are (chaps. 2—3), and the things which shall take place after these things (chaps. 4—22). Chapter 4 begins this third division. This is confirmed by the fact that the same words ("after these things") are used in 4:1 (NASB) as were used at the end of 1:19. This final division may be further divided into five subdivisions: the preface (chaps. 4—5), the judgments (chaps. 6—18), the Second Coming (chap. 19), the kingdom (chap. 20), and the heavenly city (chaps. 21—22).

When will Christ come to set up His kingdom? There are three major views concerning this. The *postmillennialists* hold that Christ's coming to this earth will be after the millennial kingdom has been already established ("post" meaning Christ's coming is *after* the millennium). According to this view, the world will see the establishment of a divine order brought about by all the people becoming saved.

A second view, *amillennialism,* holds that there is no more a future earthly kingdom of Christ than there is now ("a" meaning *no* millennium). According to this view, the promises in Scripture of an earthly kingdom refer to a time of blessedness, but not to a literal kingdom on the earth. Christ will one day come to judge both the good and evil, and then will follow the eternal state.

A third view is *premillennialism,* which holds that Christ will come before His millennial kingdom upon the earth, and He Himself will establish it ("pre" meaning Christ's coming is *before* the millennium). As we will see, the chronology of Revelation 19—20 supports this view.

Within *premillennialism,* however, there are different positions as to the church's relationship to the coming Tribulation. Some hold that the church is not taken out of the world until after the tribulation is over, and is part of the return of Christ to the earth. This is called *posttribulationalism.* Another view is that the church is taken out, or raptured, in the middle of the Tribulation. This is called *midtribulationalism.* Still another view is that the church is caught up, or raptured, before the Tribulation begins. This is known as *pretribulationalism.* Those who hold this view believe that the rapture occurs, in the Book of Revelation, at the beginning of chapter 4, at the same time John is told to "come up here" (4:1, NASB). Although people will be saved during the Tribulation, the word "church" does not occur in the Book of Revelation after 3:22, except for the benediction of the book (22:16). John does not see the church involved in the earthly events of the Tribulation.

The Throne in Heaven [4:1-11]

The One on the throne (4:1-3). The Apostle John looks right into heaven and sees the very throne of God. We find the background to this passage in the Old Testament. There the Ancient of Days has a throne ablaze with fire (Dan. 7:9-14, 22-27). This would remind John that the Lord will bring judgment on the earth and destroy many people. But does God have the right to judge the earth? Is He qualified to pour out such judgment? This chapter emphatically answers those questions.

John saw an open door (v. 1). Already there was the open door of opportunity before the church of Philadelphia (3:8). Then there was the open door of salvation (3:20). Now there was the open door of heaven, which led to the throne room of God.

John was in the spirit (v. 2). In a trance, God prepared John to see a vision, in order to receive this message from God. Now that we have the completed message, it is no longer necessary to receive such visions. This is the second vision in the Book of Revelation (cf. 1:10).

The "gap" between God and man is bridged in Jesus Christ. As a result, the believer has access to God and can come to Him as Father (Rom. 5:2). But God is also the Sovereign of the universe. This royal Ruler is the One John sees as he views the throne in heaven. It is an awesome scene, one that brings forth worship and praise.

The Lord's characteristics are represented by three stones (v. 3). The *jasper* stone is a clear stone like a diamond. This stone represents God's purity and holiness, His deity. Ruby red, the *sardius* stone signifies the sacrificial death of Christ. He paid for the sins of the world, not with silver and gold, but with His own blood. Third is the *emerald*, green in color, and a visual result of the rainbow surrounding the throne. Although we see only partial rainbows, the one around God's throne is complete. This stone represents, as did the rainbow God gave Noah, the faithfulness of God. He will do what He has promised. How privileged John was to view the throne room of God and to see representations of His deity, sacrificial love, and faithfulness!

The ones about the throne (vv. 4-5). Next, John sees those who are gathered around the throne (v. 4). Who are these beings? They might be angels or, more likely, they represent the church in heaven. There are 24 of them, symbolizing the priesthood of the church, since there were 24 orders in the Old Testament priesthood (cf. 1 Peter 2:5, 9; 1 Chron. 24).

Notice how these elders are pictured. They are sitting, showing that their earthly work is completed, although there will be much to do in heaven. They are clothed in white garments, indicating they have the righteousness of Christ, not their own filthy rags. They also have on their heads crowns of gold. The word used here means a victor's crown (Greek, *stephanous*), not a diadem. Could this picture the church already rewarded at this time?

Such a scene as God's presence is accompanied by many sights and sounds. These include lightning, thunder, and lamps of fire (v. 5). The seven spirits of God refer to the characteristics of the Holy Spirit (cf. 1:4; Isa. 11:2).

The ones before the throne (vv. 6-8). Next, John describes four living creatures that he sees before the throne. They are in the midst of a crystal clear sea that is before the throne.

Who are these beings? From John's description, they appear to be angels, similar to ones both Isaiah and Ezekiel saw (Isa. 6; Ezek. 1). Like a lion (v. 7), the first living creature illustrates the kingly characteristics of Christ pointed out in the Gospel of Matthew. The second is like a calf, representing the servant characteristics of Christ given in the Gospel of Mark. The third has a face like a man, showing the humanity of Christ emphasized by Luke. The fourth is like a flying eagle, representing the divine characteristics of Christ seen in the Gospel of John.

What do these beings do? They praise God continually in His presence (v. 8). The Almighty God, the Sovereign of the universe, has angels continually praising Him. Notice the increase of praise in these chapters (cf. 1:6; 4:8, 11; 5:13; 7:12).

The worship before the throne (vv. 9-11). Both of these

groups—the 24 elders and the living creatures—give praise, honor, and worship to the Lord. The living creatures give thanks because of who He is, because of His eternal being (v. 9).

The 24 elders give thanks because of God's creative powers (vv. 10-11). They fall down before the throne and cast their crowns at His feet. Where did they get these crowns? In the Epistles, Paul describes the Christian life as a building and believers will be rewarded according to how they have built (1 Cor. 3:11-15). Some build with perishable materials (wood, hay, stubble) while others build with permanent materials (gold, silver, precious stones). The issue is whether the believer builds his life with what God puts into it or with what he himself tries to do. The rewards take the form of crowns (cf. 1 Cor. 9:25; 1 Thes. 2:19; 2 Tim. 4:8; James 1:12; 1 Peter 5:4; Rev. 2:10; 3:11). One day believers will cast these crowns at the feet of Christ (4:10). The crowns will be used in an act of worship as the Lord receives glory, honor, and power. Embarrassment will come to some believers who have nothing to cast at the feet of Christ. How important it is for us to examine how we are building our lives now in light of this future event.

The Book in Heaven [5:1-14]

The pursuit (5:1-4). The Apostle John sees not only the throne and those around it, but also a most important book, or scroll. This is a book of judgment, and that judgment is described in the next chapter when the seals of the book are broken.

The book is held in the right hand of God (v. 1). The right hand is the place of authority and power. God, in the ultimate sense, is the One who will one day judge this world. He is the One who will show Himself victorious over sin.

The Scriptures describe many characteristics of God. He is a God of love (1 John 4:8, 16). The greatest display of His love was the giving of His Son to die for the sins of the world (John 3:16). He is also a God of holiness, as seen in the Old Testament and in the previous chapter (4:8). This means He is separate from moral evil, and He calls on us to be holy (1 Peter 1:15). He is also a God of righteousness and justice. As such, He must judge this world; He must judge sin. He hates the workers of iniquity because of their sin (Ps. 5:5). Sometimes it is difficult for us to understand why God must judge the earth. But if we remember that God is holy, righteous, and just, we can see that such judgment is consistent with His nature. God is a God of love, but not to the exclusion of His many other attributes.

This book of judgment is full. It is written inside and on the back. It is filled with the judgments that will be poured out on the earth.

The book is sealed with seven seals. It was really a scroll, rather than a book with pages as our modern books have today. There were seven seals placed throughout the book. When the first seal is broken (6:1), the judgment written on that portion of the scroll is read. When the second seal is broken (6:3), the judgment on that portion of the scroll is read. This continues until all seven seals have been broken and all the judgments contained on the scroll have been read. Much of the Book of Revelation is a record of those judgments.

Who is worthy (vv. 2-3) to open a book like this? Such a person will have to be perfect himself, for how can one judge others unless he himself is above judgment? Who in heaven, earth, or under the earth can open such a book? The search goes forth, but no one can be found.

This is the reason John weeps (literally, sobs, v. 4). No one can be found who is worthy to open the book of judgment. Then too once the judgment starts, who will be powerful enough to stop it? Can it be that God will completely destroy this world because of its sin against Him? Certainly He has the right to do so. What is going to happen?

The Person (vv. 5-7). At long last, One is found who is considered worthy to open the book. Who is this Person? How is He described?

First, He is the Lion of the tribe of Judah (v. 5). As a lion is powerful, so this One is the Sovereign King, the Lion of judgment who is able to open the book and pour out judgment on the earth. He is the offspring of humanity, the Root of David, the One who came to the earth and was born in a manger. Into His hands all judgment has been committed (John 5:22-27). This includes the judgment of the believer, the unbeliever, and the earth itself.

Second, He is a Lamb (v. 6). People are not looking for a lamb to lead them today. Seldom do athletic teams call themselves lambs. They are called bulls, bears, lions, cubs, and tigers, but not lambs. One day, however, there is coming *the Day of the Lamb,* the day in which the Lamb of God will reign in both judgment and glory. This theme will build throughout the Book of Revelation.

Notice some important facts about this Lamb. First, the Greek word used here literally means a "pet lamb." This shows the love the Father has for His Son (John 17:23, 26). Second, the Lamb is standing. Although Christ is sometimes seen seated at the right hand of the Father (Heb. 1:3), that position relates to His work on the Cross. Christ's work of salvation is completed, so He is sometimes seen as seated. But He has yet to judge the world and come as King of the earth, so here He is seen as standing.

Third, the Lamb was slain. This is in the past tense, a reference to the Cross, where Christ died to take away our sins (John 1:29). Fourth, the Lamb has seven horns. The horn is the symbol of power and these horns show the omnipotence of Christ as He judges the world. Fifth, the Lamb has seven eyes which illustrate His discernment. He will judge not only with omnipotence, but with omniscience. Sixth, the Lamb sends forth the Spirit of God into all the earth. This indicates that the coming judgment will take place throughout the world.

Who is this One who is able to judge the world? He is none other than Jesus Christ, the Lion and Lamb of God. He is the One who comes and takes the book of judgment out of the right hand of the One on the throne (v. 7). He is the only One worthy to open the book, and that opening is described in the next chapter.

The praise (vv. 8-14). This exciting scene closes with three groups giving praise to the Lord. The first group includes the redeemed, who sing to the Lord a new song (vv. 8-10).

The occasion for this song is the incense offered to the Lord (v. 8). This incense refers to the prayers of the saints, which are sent up to the Lord as a sweet-smelling savour, a sacrifice to the Lord (cf. Heb. 13:15).

What did this chorus sing? First, they sing of their redemption (v. 9). Second, they sing of their priesthood, their privilege and responsibility to represent Christ on the earth and to witness for Him. Third, they sing of their kingship (v. 10), that one day they will reign with Him on earth. In this song there is recognition of past, present, and future blessings in what God has done for them.

A second group that praises the Lord is the angels (vv. 11-12). Although we do not know how many angels there are, here the number is given as myriads of myriads (thousands of thousands).

The angels have praised the Lord many times in the past. They praised Him at Creation (Job 38:4-7) and at the first coming of Christ (Luke 2:13-14). They will also praise Him at the Second Coming (Heb. 1:6). Why do *they* praise the Lord? Because since the Lamb was slain, He is now worthy to receive worship from *all* his creation. Angels observe the outworking of God's plan in the lives of His people (1 Peter 1:12) and praise Him because of it.

The third group that praises the Lord is the entire creation (vv. 13-14). They worship both God the Father and the Lamb. As a climax to this scene, the living creatures and the 24 elders fall down and worship the Lord.

What a fitting description of the praise, thanksgiving, and worship that is given to God, who created all things and provided the gift of salvation! Is it any wonder that such a sovereign and righteous God must judge all those who have turned their backs on Him? Is it any wonder that such a God must judge a world like this? The type of judgment God is going to pour forth is described in the next chapter.

5
Famine, Wars, and Earthquakes

(Revelation 6, 8—9)

"The devastation was unbelievable, the relief direc
"There were huge rifts in the roads houses were demolished, bodies everywhere. I never believed an earthquake could cause such damage."

One survivor recalled the tense moments as the quake hit. "I dashed into our children's bedrooms," he said. "I dimly recall the details of those first seconds as my wife and I met in the hall, then raced out the front door, each with a child in our arms."

Millions of people through the centuries have directly felt the suffering and fear of earthquakes. Every two or three years a massive quake strikes somewhere in the world. The worst known earthquake occurred in China and killed nearly 1 million people. But earthquakes have hit population centers throughout the world, and the damage has resulted in untold suffering to millions.

"All of us are going to die one day," an earthquake survivor told me. "But such shock and fear can only mean someone is trying to tell us something. Could it be a message of judgment?"

A message of judgment? Although there have been many earthquakes down through history, there will be shattering ones during the end times. Famine, wars, and earthquakes will be poured out upon the earth when God moves in judgment against this world.

Such a time of judgment was first forecast by the Old Testament prophets. Zephaniah, for example, told of the houses of Jerusalem becoming desolate, the wealth being plundered, people's blood being poured out like dust (Zeph. 1:12-18). This will occur in the day of the Lord's wrath, when the whole earth will be judged.

Jesus said there would come a time on this earth of unprecedented trouble. It would be a time "such as has not occurred since the beginning of the world until now, nor ever shall" (Matt. 24:21, NASB). It would be so bad that the days would have to be cut short, or interrupted, or there would be complete annihilation of all flesh (Matt. 24:22). In other words, God would have to intervene in these judgments in order to stop them.

The most detailed description of these judgments found anywhere in Scripture is given in the Book of Revelation. In three major sections, John portrays these judgments as seal judgments (chap. 6), trumpet judgments (chaps. 8—9), and bowl, or vial, judgments (chaps. 15—16).

Before examining these judgments in detail, let's get an overview of these three major series of judgments. First, John sees the Lamb break the seals on the scroll-type book and learns of the judgment that one day will come. He sees the first seal broken and then the judgment, the second seal broken, and then the judgment, until all seven seals have been broken.

When the seventh seal is broken, the trumpets will begin to sound. In the Old Testament, trumpets were used to gather Israel together for various feasts and were signs of victory and celebration. But trumpets were also used for judgment. For instance, when the Israelites blew the trumpets after marching around the city of Jericho, the walls fell down. Jericho met judgment by means of trumpets. In a similar way, trumpets illustrate the judgment of God that one day will be poured out on the earth.

There is a telescopic effect here. When the seventh seal is opened, it *contains* the seven trumpet judgments. Following the trumpet judgments are the seven bowl judgments. Today, when we say that our cup is full, we mean our cup of blessing. One day, however, God's cup of wrath will be full and it will be spilled out on the earth.

If these are the judgments Jesus predicted, we can see why He says that unless this time is cut short, no flesh will be saved. As the judgments progress, there is a crescendo effect in that the judgments get worse. This is why the Lord must stop the judgment or the entire earth will perish. And He will stop it when He returns.

What are the judgments God will pour out on this world? Let's examine in detail the seal and trumpet judgments (chaps. 6; 8—9). We will look at the bowl judgments in a later chapter.

The Seal Judgments [6:1-17]

The first seal judgment (6:1-2). What is it that John sees in this chapter? First, he sees the Lamb take the book and break one of the seven seals (v. 1). The Lamb is none other than Jesus Christ, who alone is worthy to open the book of judgment (chap. 5). When the first seal is opened, there is the noise of thunder, indicating that judgment is coming.

The first judgment pictures someone with a bow, sitting on a white horse, going forth to conquer. Later, Jesus Christ is portrayed as One on a white horse when he comes to set up His kingdom (19:11). So, this one must be a false messiah, an antichrist, who will seek to bring false peace on the earth. Did not Jesus say that "many will come in My name"? (Matt. 24:5, NIV)

In our own day we have seen many self-proclaimed messiahs promising to relieve oppression and suffering. Most of these, however, have served their own self-interests, not the good of the people. One day an antichrist is coming who will claim to bring peace, but it will be a false peace. Instead of relieving oppression, he will serve his own interests. He will be a curse on the world.

The second seal judgment (vv. 3-4). John next sees the second seal broken and a rider on a red horse. This rider goes forth to take peace from the earth. Here is worldwide warfare in which people kill one another. But Jesus had predicted that there would be wars and rumors of wars (Matt. 24:6).

Although we hope and pray for a time of peace, throughout history there have been many wars. During a time of relative peace, however, a great war will break forth. As red symbolizes blood, so this rider will cause much bloodshed on the earth.

The third seal judgment (vv. 5-6). When the next seal is broken, John sees a rider on a black horse with a pair of scales in his hand. A voice says that there is a measure of wheat for a penny and three measures of barley for a penny.

To understand this judgment, we must understand that the word *penny* is literally a "denarius." A denarius was a day's wage for one in Caesar Augustus' army. In other words, for a day's wage, one will be able to buy only a loaf, or measure, of bread. World-wide famine will result in worldwide inflation. Although bread is expensive today, it is not as expensive as it will be. Certainly, present day inflation foreshadows such a coming Day of Judgment. Notice that in the midst of such poverty, the rich are sheltered from it. The oil and wine are not hurt (v. 6). Later, though, the rich, and even the kings of the earth, will be involved in judgment (v. 15).

The fourth seal judgment (vv. 7-8). The next rider appears on an ashen horse, a sickly pale, corpse-like color. He appears as Death itself, for he will have authority to kill with famine, pestilence, wild beasts, and with the sword. A fourth of the world's population will die during this time. Surely this will be a time of vast judgment.

These first four judgments are known as the horsemen judgments, because each one is represented by a rider on a different colored horse. But the other seals contain severe judgments too.

The fifth seal judgment (vv. 9-11). When the fifth seal is broken, John sees those who have been martyred. Why were these people martyred? One reason is because of the Word of God. At the beginning of the Tribulation, these people believed and obeyed God's Word. The other reason is because they shared that Word with others. They were martyred for their testimony.

These martyrs ask an important question, a question that Christians sometimes ask today. They want to know how long it will be before their blood is avenged on those responsible for their deaths. How long will it be before God judges the whole world? Just because God delays His judgment does not mean He will discontinue it. The answer He gives is that it will not be very long. One day He will come and thoroughly judge the earth.

The sixth seal judgment (vv. 12-17). When the sixth seal is broken, John sees great natural disturbances, disorder in the heavens and on earth. First, there is a great earthquake, then the sun becomes black, and finally the moon becomes like blood. Stars fall to the earth, perhaps a whole rash of meteorites. Even the mountains and islands are moved out of their places by these disturbances.

Some may ask if these things should be taken literally. When John pictures an event as happening, we take it that it is literally true. Sometimes he says it is *like* something else. In that case John is trying to describe what he sees in our language. For instance, notice carefully verse 12. John says there is an earthquake and something happens to the sun, moon, and stars. These events, we take it, will happen. However, John says the moon becomes *like* blood. He does not say it becomes blood, but it appears to be a blood-red color. John describes this in our language, using graphic detail to convey the "mood" of the time.

How will the people of the earth react when all this havoc

occurs? They will try to hide themselves from the wrath of the Lamb (v. 16). But rather than repent and accept Christ as Saviour, they will try to destroy themselves. Is this not true with some today?

Have you noticed the correlation between this chapter and Matthew 24? Jesus talks about an Antichrist (Matt. 24:5, the first seal), war (v. 6, the second seal), famine (v. 7, the third seal), and death (v. 7, the fourth seal). Jesus gives the outline, while John gives the details.

The judgment God is going to pour out on the earth is further described in the trumpet judgments, judgments that sound forth in Revelation 8—9. We turn to consider them now.

The Trumpet Judgments [8:1-9:21]

The preparation (8:1-6). The Lord has shown John who it is that will be able to stand during this time (chap. 7). But now when the seventh seal is broken (v. 1), there is a time of preparation, preparation which shows the importance of the prayers of God's people (v. 3).

Although it might be possible that the three series of judgments (seals, trumpets, and bowls) run concurrently, a better view is that they run sequentially, that is, they follow one another. Notice, for example, that when the seventh seal is opened, it *contains* the seven trumpet judgments which are then poured out (vv. 1-2).

What preparation is made before these judgments are given? First, there is the preparation of silence (v. 1). As there is usually a calm before the storm, so there is a calm of silence before this further storm of judgment. This silence is so that prayer may be offered to the Lord.

Second, the prayers of all the saints are sent up before God (vv. 3-5). As incense from an offering was sent up before the Lord during Old Testament times, so the prayers of these believers, mixed with incense, are offered up before God. These prayers are accompanied by thunder, lightning, and an earthquake (v. 5).

Third, there is an answer to the prayers (v. 6). This answer is the judgment that follows, for God must judge this world. The angels prepare to sound the trumpets of judgment.

The first trumpet judgment (v. 7). When the first trumpet is sounded, John sees the judgment taking place on the earth. This is a judgment against the *vegetation* of the earth. One third of the trees and grass is burned up. If one third of such vegetation is removed from production, it will cause great world suffering.

The second trumpet judgment (vv. 8-9). This judgment is against the *transportation systems* of the earth. It is a judgment against the sea, creatures, and ships. Because of this judgment, one third of the sea becomes blood, one third of the sea creatures die, and one third of the ships are destroyed.

The third trumpet judgment (vv. 10-11). When the third trumpet is sounded, there is great judgment on the *sanitation* of the earth. This judgment involves "wormwood," a very bitter and intoxicating plant. It is used in the Old Testament for divine chastisement (Deut. 29:18; Lam. 3:15). The impure water resulting from this judgment causes the death of many people. Although there is some water pollution today, it is mild compared to the pollution that will be caused by this judgment.

The fourth trumpet judgment (vv. 12-13). This judgment is against the *heavenly bodies*. A third part of the sun, moon, and stars is smitten so that a third of the day and a third of the night are darkened. In a day of great interest in solar energy, one can easily see the devastating effect of such a judgment. John is also warned that there are three woes to come, the last three blasts of the trumpet (v. 13).

The fifth trumpet judgment (9:1-12). The fifth trumpet judgment is a judgment of *pestilence*, namely, a horde of locusts that come against the peoples of the earth. Notice some important facts about these locusts.

First is their abode (vv. 1-3). They come from the bottomless pit, the abyss of the earth. The one who has a key to this place is an evil angel, Satan's chief of staff (v. 1). When he opens this place of torment, smoke rises out of it, like out of a great furnace (v. 2). This is the unseemly place of the earth. The locusts appear out of the smoke and are given great power (v. 3). These are locusts of judgment which will torment the peoples of the world.

Second is their purpose (vv. 4-6). They were first told what they could not do, as Satan was told by God what he could not do when he attacked Job. These locusts cannot hurt the grass, or any green thing, or any tree, or those who are sealed by God (v. 4). What, then, can they do? They can torment those who have not been sealed for five months (v. 5). The locusts' torment is so terrible that people would rather die than live.

Third is their appearance (vv. 7-10). Notice the word "like" in this description. John illustrates their appearance in our terms. They are unique beings, specially prepared for the torment they give. Their shapes are like horses; on their heads are crowns like gold; faces like the faces of men; hair like women's hair; teeth like lion's teeth; breastplates like iron; tails like scorpions.

Fourth is their king (vv. 11-12). As there are different ranks among good angels, so there are different ranks among evil angels. These locusts have a king over them (v. 11). The name of this king, in both Hebrew and Greek, means "destroyer." His purpose is to destroy the people of the earth. He will use these locusts to aid him.

The sixth trumpet judgment (9:13-21). This is a judgment of *death*, a judgment in which a third of mankind is killed (v. 15).

John hears the command from the golden altar in heaven for four angels to be released. These angels had been bound at the Euphrates River, and are now released because a great army is coming from that eastern direction.

This army, the largest ever recorded in history or prophecy, numbers 200 million people. Their purpose is to kill a third of mankind and they will do so. In addition to the army, there is fire and smoke and brimstone coming from the mouths of demon-like creatures. Those who are not killed by these plagues will not repent even though they have witnessed such judgment of God. Does this not show the hardness of people's hearts? Even in the Day of Judgment, they will not repent.

These judgments are devastating. They cause great havoc on the earth and many people die. Consider the effects of just two of these judgments. Notice the fourth seal judgment (6:8) when a fourth of the earth is killed. This means one fourth of the world's population will be cut off. Then look at the sixth trumpet judgment (9:15) when a third of the remaining people is killed. If we add these numbers together, we find that half of the world's population is killed by just two judgments. Faced with these facts, we can see why Jesus said that unless these days were cut short, no flesh would be saved (Matt. 24:22). This will be a time of great tribulation.

Although the world may seem bad today, it is not nearly as bad as it one day will be. This is why it is so important that we are involved in God's program today, that of building His church. We are privileged to have such opportunities and we must use them for God's purpose and glory. May we be faithful to the tasks He has given us.

But in such a time of coming judgment, will anyone be able to stand for the Lord and serve Him? We turn to this important subject now.

6
Who
Are
the
144,000?

(Revelation 7)

In a small rural area lives a hardworking farmer who has lived a simple life for 23 years. He rises each day before dawn and works until well after sunset. When asked, "Why do you work so hard?" his strange answer is, "I am one of the 144,000!"

In a Midwestern city there's a building contractor who is known by even business associates as a very religious person. He is faithful to his work, builds good houses, gives a fair price. When asked, "What is your religion?" his strange answer is, "I am one of the 144,000!"

In an Ozark town lives a family that has gone from one church to another. In desperation they have decided not to go to any church at all but to stay home and listen to a "television church" originating from a western state. They like the smooth format of the program, the charm of the speaker, but especially what he says. Time after time, he declares that they are part of the 144,000!

Many people believe they are part, or will be, part of, the 144,000. Some radio and television speakers believe the United States is one of the lost tribes of Israel and therefore part of this select group. Others believe they are living during the end times and are therefore part of this group God plans to use. Still others, not wanting to miss out on any spiritual blessing, are curious about what this group is and their possible relationship to it.

Who are the 144,000? This is one of the most talked about and controversial prophetic subjects. As with all other doctrines, it is important to examine carefully what the Scriptures teach concerning this unique group. We find the answers in Revelation 7.

God will pour out vast judgment on the earth during the coming Tribulation Period. Seal judgments, trumpet judgments, and bowl judgments will plague the world within a short span of time. Many people will be killed and many others will be tormented. Who will be able to stand against such wrath of God? Who will be able to live during this time? These strategic questions are answered in Revelation 7.

The Remnant of Israel [7:1-8]

The scene (7:1-3). After seeing the seals broken on the book of judgment (chap. 6), John beholds another scene. He sees four angels standing at the four corners of the earth (v. 1). What are these angels doing? They are holding back the four winds of the earth so that the winds will not blow on the earth. These winds represent the universal judgment that will come on the world (cf. Dan. 7:2; Matt. 24:31; Rev. 14:18; 16:5). The angels are holding back this judgment so John can see who it is that can stand during this time.

What else does John see? He sees another angel, this one coming from the east (v. 2). This angel tells the other angels not to hurt the world until the servants of God are sealed (v. 3). The angel has God's seal and he is to seal God's special servants who are living during this time. But why is a seal used? What is its significance? In the past, seals were used for many different purposes. For example, a seal might be used for secrecy. When a person mailed a letter, he sealed it so no one else could view its contents. Or a seal might signify a completed transaction. When a promise or covenant was made, the use of a seal on the document certified it. One of the most common uses of a seal was for protection. The seal, a mark of wax, assured that a letter or package would arrive at its destination. Then too, a seal showed ownership. A special seal's mark showed that an item belonged to a certain individual.

These people are sealed for two important reasons. First, they are sealed to show ownership, God's ownership. These are servants, bond-servants of the Lord, and the seal shows that important fact.

Second, they also are sealed for protection, protection from the judgment of God. It is during the time of the Tribulation that they are witnesses for the Lord. With judgment falling all around, it will be easy for these servants to be killed before their ministry is completed. This is why God seals them so they are protected from the physical harm that otherwise might come to them. For this reason the angel says not to harm the world until these servants have been sealed.

This seal will be visible, for the servants of God are sealed "on their foreheads" (v. 3, NASB). What this seal will look like, we do not know. It will not look like the mark of the beast, which will be during this time in another connection (13:16). This seal will be for these people of God, not for those who are worshiping the beast. Later, as judgment comes, God will command that these people, who have been especially sealed, should not be harmed (9:4). The seal will be visible so that this command can be followed.

The sealed (vv. 4-8). Who are these people about whom so much has been written and about whom so much confusion exists? The Scriptures clearly tell us who they are. Let's carefully examine the evidence.

First, they are believers, not unbelievers. They are called bond-servants of God (v. 3). Their purpose is to minister for the Lord, so they must be believers.

Second, they are on earth during the Tribulation. They are standing during the time when God is judging the earth. Although believers may experience suffering today, they are not witnessing the destruction that one day will come on this world. It is then that these sealed servants will minister for the Lord.

Third, they are a limited number. John specifically notes that the number is 144,000 (v. 4). This does not include all who will be saved during this time, but only those who are sealed, or protected, by God. There is no reason to take this number as anything but literal.

Fourth, they are Jews (v. 5). There are 12,000 of these sealed servants from each of the 12 tribes of Israel. This means that there are no Gentiles in this group.

Each of the 12 tribes of Israel is listed (vv. 5-8), but the tribe of Levi is substituted for the tribe of Dan and the tribe of Joseph is substituted for the tribe of Ephraim. Why are Dan and Ephraim omitted? God is probably chastising them because of their fondness for wickedness and idolatry (cf. Deut. 29:18-21; Gen. 49:17; Jud. 18; 1 Kings 12:25-30). However, they will have an important place in the millennial kingdom and will worship God there (Ezek. 48:1-7). Here Levi, the Old Testament priestly tribe is substituted for Dan since the Old Testament priesthood ended with the death of Christ and there is no land involved in this passage. Joseph, Ephraim's father, is substituted for him.

Fifth, they have a visible seal on their foreheads (v. 3). This is so that they can be easily identified by God's angels when judgment comes.

Although many Gentiles today may wish to be part of this special group, it is clear that they are not part of the 144,000. Believers today do have important ministries for the Lord, however, and they are to be faithful in carrying out those responsibilities.

How will these Jewish evangelists, the 144,000, come to Christ? If the church has been raptured before this dreadful time of tribulation, who will be left to lead the 144,000 to the Lord?

Although the church will have been taken out of the world before this time, this does not mean there will be no witness for God on the earth. There will still be Gospel literature, tracts, and, of course, the Scriptures themselves. There probably will also be taped Gospel radio and television programs giving forth the Word of God. Once some of these Jewish evangelists come to Christ, they in turn will lead many others to the Saviour. The church may be gone, but God's witness will continue on a temporary basis through other means.

The Revival of All Nations [7:9-17]

The multitude (7:9). Who will the 144,000 lead to the Lord? John speaks of some of these people in this next section as he describes a vast multitude that will be saved during the Tribulation.

That this great multitude is different from the 144,000 is clear for several reasons. First, it is an *innumerable* multitude, whereas the 144,000 is a specific number. Second, it is made up of all nations, in contrast to the 144,000 who are Jews. Third, it is a group that comes *out of* the Tribulation, whereas the 144,000 were sealed servants *in* the Tribulation. This group is placed after the 144,000 in this chapter because many, if not all of them will have been won to the Lord through the ministry of the 144,000. The 144,000 will be special Jewish messengers, divinely protected, who will go throughout the whole earth as ministers of God. As soon as some from this multitude come to Christ, they too will be witnesses for Him. But since they have not been sealed, as have the 144,000, they will quickly be put to death by the forces of the Antichrist. That is why John sees them in heaven, not on the earth.

How does this multitude of believers from all nations appear before the Lord? First, they are clothed in white robes. Such clothing shows they have received God's righteousness, a righteousness that is perfect and pure, a righteousness that is not their own. Second, they have palm branches in their hands. This illustrates their continued praise of the Lord.

The message (vv. 10-12). What does this multitude say as they face the Lord in heaven? They praise God for their salvation. It is because the Lord has sent His Son, and the Lamb has died for them, that they can have deliverance from sin, full and free.

When this multitude praises the Lord, the angels, 24 elders, and living creatures also honor Him. They fall on their faces in worship, and praise Him for His wisdom, power, and eternality. Angels, of course, do not personally experience salvation, but they do learn from believers. They also know of the wisdom and power of God through their own ministry for Him. God alone is to be worshiped, and here both angels and redeemed people worship Him.

The meaning (vv. 13-17). "Who is this great multitude and what is the meaning of this heavenly scene?" One of the 24 elders asks John this question. When John wonders about this, the elder answers the question.

They are those who have come out of the Great Tribulation (v. 14), Tribulation saints. Although there will be much destruction and judgment during the Tribulation, many people will be saved anyway.

What will these people do? Throughout eternity they will be able to serve the Lord unhindered (v. 15). Many believers would like to serve the Lord completely today, but distractions hinder them from doing so. These people will be able to serve the Lord without any distractions whatsoever. The grace of God is shown in that He will protect them; He will spread His tabernacle over them. Although these people will not be protected during the Tribulation, as will be the 144,000, God will protect them throughout eternity. He will shelter them forever. They will have complete satisfaction too, for they will never again hunger or thirst (v. 16). In fact, they no longer will have the sun beating down on them.

Why is this? It is because it is the Day of the Lamb. The Lamb of God will not only unleash judgment during the Tribulation, but He will also pour out blessing during the Millennium and in the eternal state. He will be their portion; He will be their provision.

What blessing will the Lamb give? First, He will be their Shepherd (v. 17). He will guide and care for them. As a human shepherd takes care of all the needs of his sheep, so this divine Shepherd will care for His own.

Second, He will give them abundant life. He will guide them to the springs of the Water of Life. The goal of the Christian life is not only deliverance from sin but also fellowship with God forever. Throughout eternity believers will have this fellowship as they enjoy the very Source of their spiritual life, the Springs of Living Water. They will not merely exist, but *live* throughout eternity. And that life will be a vital and vibrant life with the Lord.

Third, He will comfort them. He will wipe every tear from their eyes. There will be no suffering or misery in heaven. As Psalm 23 speaks of the Shepherd's care and concern for His sheep, so this passage shows the Lamb's care and concern for His sheep throughout eternity. Indeed, it will be *the Day of the Lamb*.

We can be the objects of that care and concern today. God, who gave His Son to die for unbelievers, has done even more for believers. He is concerned about us and cares for our every problem and need. Should we not therefore enjoy the fellowship and help He gives us today?

7
Witnesses, Woman, and War

(Revelation 10—12)

"Ladies and gentlemen," the evening newscaster announced "we have an unusual report from the city of Jerusalem. Two men there have reportedly been prophesying for the past three-and-one-half years while clothed in sackcloth. Both of them had been doing spectacular feats, such as making fire come out of their mouths. These two were also said to be able in some way to hold back rain from the earth. But they were recently killed and their bodies have been lying in the street of Jerusalem for several days. We go there now for an on-the-spot report."

"Thank you, Walter. The scene here is very tense and has been for the last three-and-one-half days. The people have not permitted the bodies of these prophets to be buried, but have rejoiced over them and have celebrated their deaths. We are at the scene now.

"Wait a minute, Walter. Someone said the bodies are starting to move! It's hard to believe what is happening here. Maybe if we move in closer, we can see better.

"Look! They are standing on their feet! The crowd is falling back in amazement . . . . I can't believe what I've just seen! The two prophets rose right up into heaven while we all watched!''

One day that very scene will take place, for it is recorded in Revelation 11. Two witnesses will come to earth, minister for the Lord, be killed, and then come back to life and will be taken right up into heaven. It will be a spectacular time, one in which God shows His power over the forces of evil.

We have seen how God will pour out fierce judgment on the earth during the Tribulation Period (chaps. 6; 8—9). We have also seen that there will be 144,000 specially sealed Jewish evangelists during this time and that many from every tribe and nation will turn to the Lord (chap. 7). During the Tribulation Period, other events also will take place on the earth. Several of these events are written in a book John describes (chap. 10). Some events involve the two witnesses who will minister for the Lord (chap. 11). And some include persecution of the nation Israel (chap. 12). We now turn to a careful consideration of these events.

The Little Book [10:1-11]

The angel and the book (10:1-7). John sees several different books that he describes in Revelation. He sees a book of judgment sealed with seven seals (chap. 6). He sees a book of works when unbelievers are judged before the Lord (20:12). He sees the Book of Life, in which are recorded the names of those who have believed (20:12). Here he sees an opened little book (10:2) which records some of the events that occur when judgment falls on the world.

Who holds this book? From the description given, it might seem that this is Christ Himself. This person is from heaven, has been clothed with a cloud, has a rainbow upon his head, has a face like the sun and feet like pillars of fire (v. 1). But he could also be an important angel and is so identified by John (v. 5). Also, there is no reason for Christ to appear on earth at this time in the chronology of Revelation. His Second Coming is not until later.

This angel's right foot is on the sea and his left is on the earth, illustrating the universal appeal of the message. He cries with a loud voice, accompanied by seven peals of thunder (v. 3).

What message do these voices of thunder give? No one knows, for John is told to seal the message (v. 4). Others also were sometimes told to seal messages they had received from God (cf. Dan. 8:26; 12:4, 9).

The scene continues with the angel lifting his hand to heaven and declaring that there should no longer be any delay (v. 6), that is, any delay of judgment. When God acts, He acts quickly.

The sounding of the seventh angel is important for it is then that God's mystery is finished (v. 7). This mystery, or secret, is the total purpose of God throughout human history. What God is doing and will do reaches its climax in the millennial kingdom set up on the earth after the seventh trumpet is sounded.

John and the book (vv. 8-11). The action now shifts from what John sees to what he does. He is told to take the book and eat it. After doing so, he finds that it makes his stomach bitter but his mouth sweet as honey (v. 9).

What is the meaning of John's two reactions? The bitterness shows that the coming judgment will be bitter. God's judgment, though necessary, is always distasteful. The sweetness shows that the judgment soon will be over. The judgment, though severe, will be quick.

When John takes the book, he finds that what the angel said is exactly what happens (v. 10). Then John is told that he must prophesy "again" (v. 11). Can this mean he must describe the events of the Tribulation a second time?

The events of Revelation 6—19 may be strictly chronological. But a better view is that, although the three series of judgments (seals, trumpets, bowls) are chronological, John outlines the major events of this time period in Revelation 6—11, and then goes back over this same Tribulation Period a second time in obedience to the command to prophesy again (10:11). When he describes the period the second time (in Rev. 12—19), he spotlights the "actors" who will then be prominent—Israel, the Antichrist, the Harlot, etc.

The Two Witnesses [11:1-19]

The times of the Gentiles (11:1-2). What was the message of the little book? Part of it may be what is recorded in these next chapters.

John is told to measure the temple of God with a measuring rod (v. 1). This temple is the Tribulation temple that will be taken over by the Antichrist (Matt. 24:15; 2 Thes. 2:4).

John is told to measure the temple, the altar area, and the inner court. The outer court, the place of the Gentiles, he is not to measure, for they will continue to be in dominion in Jerusalem for another 42 months. Previously, Jesus defined the times of the Gentiles as that time when Gentiles would trample down the city of Jerusalem (Luke 21:24). Although Gentiles may not own the Holy City all of this time, they will have dominion over the city until the second coming of Christ. It is then that Christ, the Stone cut out without hands, will destroy all Gentile power and rule the world Himself (Dan. 2:44). By measuring only what is relevant to Israel in the temple, John focuses attention on Israel and the city of Jerusalem in this passage.

The two witnesses (vv. 3-14). Sometime during the Tribulation, two witnesses prophesy for 42 months. They are clothed in sackcloth, a sign of mourning (v. 3).

They are compared to two olive trees and two lampstands. As olive trees produce oil for light and lampstands give off light, so these witnesses produce God's light for a dark world. They are witnesses for God to do His will in that day.

When do these people witness for the Lord? Although the 42 months of 11:2 come at the end of the Tribulation, the 42 months (1,260 days) of 11:3 come before then, perhaps at the beginning of the Tribulation. We know this because certain events must take place on the earth *after* these witnesses complete their ministry. If this is true, their ministry coincides with that of the 144,000. These two men are special witnesses of God to bring an entire city to sense God's coming judgment.

How is their ministry authenticated? During Old Testament times, prophets of God had their ministry authenticated by miracles from heaven. These witnesses also perform miracles. They cause fire to come out of their mouths, cause rain to cease, turn the waters to blood, and smite the earth with plagues (vv. 5-6).

On the basis of these miracles, some hold that these witnesses are Elijah and Moses. The first two miracles are similar to ones Elijah did while the last two were performed by Moses. Others believe the two may be Enoch and Elijah, since both Enoch and Elijah were translated directly to heaven. Perhaps the best approach is to accept what the Scriptures record, that they are unnamed. Just because the miracles are similar to those of Elijah and Moses does not mean that these witnesses are Elijah and Moses. And just because Enoch and Elijah were translated does not mean that they need to return to perform such an end-time ministry. God can easily use two people during the Tribulation to accomplish His purpose.

What happens to these witnesses? When they finish their testimony, the beast that comes out of the bottomless pit, makes war with them and kills them (v. 7). This is the first mention, in Revelation, of this beast who will be fully described in Revelation 13. His purpose is to do the work of Satan and to make war with whoever serves God, including these two witnesses.

The bodies of these dead witnesses lie in the street in the middle of the city of Jerusalem (v. 8). This strategic city of world importance is then known as Sodom because of its spiritual bankruptcy. Jews, who have received so much from the hand of God, then bring great dishonor to Him.

The people of the world view these bodies for three-and-one-half days (v. 9). How do they do this? The only way for so many to see will be through some electronic means like television.

Although Jewish law says that the dead should be buried on the day they die, the people will not allow the authorities to put the witnesses' bodies in graves.

What does the world do when they see these bodies? Instead of sorrow and bereavement, they "rejoice over them and make merry" (v. 10). In fact, they will send gifts to one another, a sign of great celebration. This is the only time during the Tribulation when rejoicing is mentioned, and it has to do with the persecution and affliction of others.

After three-and-one-half days, the two witnesses are resurrected, stand up, and ascend into heaven (vv. 11-12). This is followed by a great earthquake with devastating results (v. 13). One tenth of Jerusalem falls and 7,000 people die. The rest of the people are terrified and give glory to God. This does not mean they are saved, but rather that they are amazed at God's miracles. Was this not also true at Christ's first coming? There were many then who wanted to see His miracles but would not accept Him. How much better to receive the One to whom the miracles point!

The seventh trumpet judgment (vv. 15-19). The long interlude between the sixth and seventh trumpet judgments is now complete. The seventh trumpet sounds.

When the trumpet sounds, an announcement of the kingdom is made (v. 15). *Even though other events must take place before the kingdom is realized, the declaration of that kingdom is now made.*

Christ will establish His kingdom on the earth and His rule will be forever. This is why the 24 elders fall on their faces in an act of worship before Him (vv. 16-17). This is also why the nations are enraged (v. 18). They know that this is a time of judgment for unbelievers who are cast into the lake of fire. But it is also a time when God rewards those who have served Him. This is then an announcement of Christ's coming to reign on the earth and judgment for those who do not know Him.

After this announcement, John introduces the next subject.

The Woman and the War [12:1-17]

The woman (12:1-6). The subject of this chapter begins with 11:19, when John sees the temple and ark of the covenant in heaven, accompanied by lightning, thunder, an earthquake, and a hailstorm. The temple and ark of the covenant are of central concern to Israel, and the natural disorders show the persecution and judgment that will come to that nation. How this will happen is the next subject to be discussed.

John sees a great sign in heaven, a woman with a crown of 12 stars (v. 1). Who is this woman? Some people think she is the Virgin Mary, but the woman continues on the earth after the ascension of Christ (vv. 5-6). Others believe the woman is the church, but there is nothing to support this view either. The church was not in existence before Pentecost as is the woman (cf. v. 5). Nor does the church give birth to Christ as does the woman (cf. v. 5).

The woman must therefore represent the nation of Israel, the nation which gave birth to Christ (Isa. 9:6; Micah 5:2-3; Rom. 9:5). Also, Israel is previously pictured as a woman in Scripture (Isa. 47:7-9; 54:1-6; 66:7-8; Hosea 2:16). In addition, Israel is related to the sun, moon, and stars (Gen. 37:9-10). We see that the immediate context of the passage supports this interpretation, for there are many Jewish symbols. These include the temple, Ark of the Covenant, and the very idea of a sign.

But there is another person as well, the dragon who has 7 heads and 10 horns (v. 3). This is none other than Satan himself, for he is identified as such later in the chapter (v. 9). The dragon draws one-third of the stars, or demonic angels, to the earth (v. 4). His whole purpose has been and will be to destroy the Man Child.

If the woman is Israel and the dragon is Satan, who is the child? He is none other than Christ, the One who will rule all nations (v. 5), the One who was caught up unto God in the Ascension. During the Tribulation, Satan will be persecuting the woman, the nation Israel. In that day she will flee to the wilderness, to a place especially prepared for her by God (v. 6).

The war (vv. 7-17). Throughout history, there have been many wars on earth, but one day there will be a war in heaven. This war will be fought between the good and evil angels—Michael and his angels against Satan and his angels (v. 7).

The result of this war is that Satan and his angels lose and are thrown down to the earth (v. 9). They will no longer be able to inhabit the heavenly places where they are today (cf. Eph. 6:12). The fact that Satan knows he has but a short time to do his work before Christ returns (v. 12) may be the reason that the second half of the Tribulation Period is so much more violent than the first half.

How are believers at this time to overcome Satan, the one who has accused them before the throne of God? (v. 10) Believers overcome him by the blood of the Lamb and the word of their testimony (v. 11). Isn't this the same way we overcome Satan today? John wrote, "Greater is He that is in you than he that is in the world" (1 John 4:4).

During the Tribulation, Satan will persecute the nation of Israel, the woman who brought forth Christ (v. 13). How long will this go on? It will be for time (one), times (two), and half a time (one-half)—or a total of three-and-one-half years (v. 14). This will be the last three-and-one-half years (42 months) of the Tribulation Period.

What will happen to Israel when she is persecuted? She will go into the wilderness, to her place (cf. vv. 6, 14). Although it is not specifically mentioned, this may be the rock-fortress Petra, the old capital city of Edom. In any event, God will miraculously protect this people by causing the earth itself to open and swallow the vengeance Satan will pour out (v. 16).

During this time, however, Satan will not only persecute Israel, but also all believers. He will afflict all who keep God's commandments (v. 17). But believers will be victorious over Satan (v. 11) even as they can be victorious over him today. How important it is to live for Christ now, knowing that Satan can be defeated when we continue to trust the Lord day by day!

8
The Dragon, Beast, and False Prophet

(Revelation 13)

Impossible! Absolutely impossible! Yet, there it was!

Hundreds and hundreds of bodies wearing white T-shirts, blue dresses, tan slacks lying on the ground as the plane swooped down. There were children still in parents' arms and couples holding each other. But no one moved!

This was the scene at the mass suicide of the Peoples Temple of Jonestown. There, in the jungles of Guyana, on the northern coast of South America, over 900 people died after being exhorted to commit suicide by their leader. They drank a concoction of potassium cyanide and potassium chloride, flavored by strawberry Flavour-aide, then keeled over. The world was horrified when it heard the details of this slaughter.

How was it possible for Jim Jones to have such a hold on so many people? James Warren Jones grew up in an Indiana town where early in his life he had a preoccupation with death. He conducted funerals for all sorts of animals—mice, cats, dogs, everything. When he grew older, he began his own church, the Community National Church, which became the Peoples Temple.

Later, he moved the church to Redwood Valley, north of San Francisco, and then to the country of Guyana.

As his church grew—up to 20,000, Jones claimed—the services became more and more strange. He "healed" people by pretending to take out of them cancers which were actually bloody chicken gizzards. Said his associate, the Rev. Ross Case, "Jim stopped calling himself the reincarnation of Jesus and started calling himself God. He said he was the actual God who made the heavens and earth" ("Messiah from the Midwest," *Time*, December 4, 1978, p. 27).

Jones demanded all his members' money and property, and assembled a fortune estimated at $15 million. He commanded his followers to carry pictures of himself to ward off evil. This progression downward was foreshadowed when once, as a young preacher, Jones threw his Bible to the floor and yelled, "Too many people are looking at this instead of me!" ("The Emperor Jones," *Newsweek*, December 4, 1978, p. 56)

One day another person will come on the world scene, much like this "messiah" from the Midwest. This person of the future will call himself God and will seek the worship of the world. He too will inflict brutal beatings as he makes war with the saints. And the world then will accept him just as Jim Jones' followers accepted their leader.

This will happen during the Tribulation Period, the time when the judgments described in the Book of Revelation are poured out on the earth. This person will be a political leader, a dictator of a large group of nations. He will also be a military leader, one who will lead nations into a devastating world war. He will have religious ambitions, for he will seek to be worshiped by the world. This person is the one whom many call the Antichrist.

The word *antichrist* is used only four times in Scripture (1 John 2:18, 22; 4:3; 2 John 7). There are, however, many other descriptions of this person. He is called the "little horn" (Dan. 7), the king of fierce countenance (Dan. 8), the prince that shall come (Dan. 9), the willful king (Dan. 11), and the man of sin (2 Thes. 2). In Revelation 13 he is seen as the beast that comes out of the sea (13:1).

During the Tribulation, another person will be associated with the Antichrist, one who will help the Antichrist gain the worship of the world. Called the false prophet, he is the beast that comes out of the land (Rev. 13:11).

Behind these two persons is the one who empowers them, Satan himself. He is called the dragon or the devil, and his goals and purposes have been outlined throughout the Scriptures. Revelation 13 focuses on his scheme of using these two beasts to accomplish his purposes during the Tribulation Period. What will happen during this time?

The Coming World Dictator [13:1-10]

His person (13:1-3). This chapter opens with John standing on the seashore. What does he see? He sees a strange beast coming up out of the sea. Here God teaches literal truth concerning what will happen on the earth, but He uses symbols to illustrate characteristics of this beast. For example, the sea represents the nations of the earth (Rev. 17:15; Isa. 57:20). This beast will arise from the nations (i.e., he will be a Gentile), and will have worldwide influence.

How else is this person described? He has 10 horns, 7 heads, 10 diadems, and blasphemous names. The horns illustrate the authority, power, and nations of this beast. Horns later, are identified as kings or kingdoms (17:12). This one is the leader of a 10-nation confederacy, a 10-nation federation. He is a political leader. The fact that these horns have diadems further shows the beast's kingly nature.

This confederacy is not a good one, for the beast's authority is divided; he has only 7, not 10 heads. On the heads are blasphemous names, blasphemous against God. The beast is against God, not for God. He is anti, or against, Christ.

John further identifies this beast as one who is like a leopard, a bear, and a lion (v. 2). What do these animals represent?

Centuries earlier, the Prophet Daniel gave the background for this passage. You remember the episode in which Daniel saw four animals or beasts that came up out of the sea (Dan. 7:1-7). The first beast was like a lion, which illustrated the ancient Babylonian Empire. The second beast resembled a bear, indicating the Medo-Persian Empire. The third beast was like a leopard, showing the Greek Empire, which, under Alexander the Great, rapidly gained world dominion. The fourth beast was simply described as "dreadful and terrible" (Dan. 7:7), illustrating the Roman Empire.

Daniel went a step further, however. He saw that the fourth beast, the Roman Empire, had 10 horns (Dan. 7:7). In other words, one day a revived Roman Empire, a confederacy of 10 nations will arise on the world scene. Although the old Roman Empire disintegrated in A.D. 476, it will one day be reestablished. Some believe the European Common Market may be a foreshadowing of such a revived Roman Empire.

The leader of this 10-nation confederacy is the Antichrist, the little horn of Daniel (Dan. 7:8) and the first beast of Revelation 13. He has the ingredients of the previous world empires within him. For instance, when the Medo-Persian Empire (the bear) took over the Babylonian Empire (the lion), it engulfed that previous empire. When the Greek Empire (the leopard) took over the Medo-Persian empire (the bear), it seized the whole previous empire. When the Roman Empire (no name) took over the Greek Empire (the leopard), it engulfed that empire. So it is that the Antichrist, the leader of the final form of the Roman Empire has the characteristics of the previous empires within him. This is why the leopard, bear, and lion are mentioned in Revelation 13:2. The Antichrist is a political leader.

Where does this world dictator get his power? From none other than the dragon, Satan himself (v. 2). It is the devil who energizes this world leader. The Antichrist is Satan's ruler on the earth. In that day God will show what will happen to the world if it is left to run by itself. The Antichrist embodies Satan's program and purpose.

To get the world to follow this beast, a great miracle occurs. The Antichrist is actually slain and Satan heals him (v. 3). Because of this event, the whole world is amazed and follows him. Satan will try to counterfeit the work of God then even as he does today.

His performance (vv. 4-7). What does this beast do? First, he accepts the worship of the world (v. 4). But only God is to be worshiped. This is what John learns later when he tries to worship the angel that shows him many things (22:8). Yet, both the Antichrist and Satan, the one who gives him authority, are worshiped by the world.

Second, he blasphemes God (vv. 5-6). He wants nothing to do with God; he only wants himself. He usurps the authority and worship of God. One who accepts worship blasphemes God by such an act. The Antichrist, however, not only openly blasphemes God but also all that is associated with God. This includes His name, His tabernacle, and those who dwell in heaven. All things and people that bear the name of God, Antichrist is against. This is why he is called Antichrist, for the word means "one who is against Christ."

Third, he reigns for 42 months (v. 5). This is three-and-one-half years, or the last half of the Tribulation Period. Revealed at the beginning of the Tribulation, he makes a peace covenant with the nation Israel (Dan. 9:27). It takes him the first three-and-one-half years to build his kingdom. From the middle of the Tribulation to the end, however, is the time when he is in control. It is then that he has authority to act for 42 months.

Fourth, he makes war with the saints (v. 7). He tries to stamp out all worship of God. He persecutes all who name the name of God during this time, and tries to overcome them. These are the believers who have been saved under the ministry of the 144,000 and the two witnesses. In that day it will be hard not to worship the Antichrist, for he will have worldwide influence. Authority will be given him over the peoples of the world. But God will still have believers then, and their lives will demonstrate their faith.

His people (vv. 8-10). Who are the people that follow this beast and worship him? They are unbelievers, the unsaved (v. 8).

God reveals two important characteristics of these people. First, they are earth dwellers, those who remain or abide on the earth. For them, the earth is their goal. Their hope and trust is wrapped up in this world. As believers abide in Christ, these people "abide" in the earth.

Second, these people's names are not written in the Book of Life. This is not a book of existence, but rather of life as God sees it. The names in this book show those who have spiritual life with the Lord. The basis of this life is the Lamb who was slain, the One who paid the penalty for sin. But the beast's followers have not accepted Christ as Saviour; they have not accepted the work of the Lamb.

What happens to these unbelievers? These people are destined for captivity. They kill with the sword, and what they do to others is eventually done to them (v. 10). God stops the madness of this world; He stops the persecution brought by the Antichrist. Assurance of this sustains believers during this critical period. They realize that God will win, and they continue to trust Him.

Is it not the same with us today? There are great injustices in the world, and many take advantage of those who trust the Lord. But God will one day right all the wrongs; He will make all things right. We therefore need to trust in Him and what He will do rather than finding fault with others. The Lord will accomplish His purposes.

The Coming False Prophet [13:11-18]

Who he is (13:11). In addition to the beast that comes out of the sea during the Tribulation, there also is a beast that comes out of the earth or land. Who is this one?

First, he is out of the land, probably a reference to the land of Israel. If so, this person is a Jew, whereas the first beast is a Gentile. This may explain why Jews follow the first beast. They are more likely to do so if led by one of their own.

Second, he is like a lamb. Since the previous reference to a lamb in this chapter is to Christ (v. 8), this beast is a counterfeit of Christ. He is involved with religious matters, especially with the worship of the first beast. This is why he is called the false prophet.

Third, he speaks like a dragon. In other words, the same dragon, or Satan, that energizes the first beast also energizes this beast. Both of these beasts do the work of Satan and seek to accomplish his purpose. The first beast is the one who is most prominent throughout Scripture, but this second beast is his helper, and tries to get the world to obey him.

What he does (vv. 12-18). What is it that this second beast, the false prophet, does? The apostle explains this in the rest of chapter 13. His main work is to get all who dwell on the earth to worship the first beast (v. 12). He is a false prophet who tries to direct attention and worship to another. How does he do this? He is controlled by Satan (v. 11), and does great wonders and miracles that authenticate him as a prophet (v. 13).

Many believe that God alone has power. A study of Scripture, however, shows that Satan is also powerful and uses his power to counterfeit the work of God. For instance, when Moses and Aaron faced Pharaoh in Egypt, Aaron threw his staff on the ground and it became a serpent. The sorcerers and magicians of Egypt threw their staffs on the ground and the staffs also became serpents. But what happened? Aaron's staff swallowed up the staffs of those who were trying to counterfeit the work of God (Ex. 7:12). It is not merely a matter of power, but of the greatness of the power. God's power is *greater* than the power of Satan (1 John 4:4).

What miracle does this false prophet perform? He calls down fire from heaven (v. 13). He does that which Elijah did in the Old Testament and which one of the two witnesses do during the Tribulation. He is a false prophet but will seek authentication as a true prophet (cf. 2 Kings 1:10; Mal. 4:5-6).

He also deceives the people of the earth by making a great image to the first beast (v. 14). This is a model of the first beast, a beautiful display of himself. Man always likes to think well of himself.

Moreover, the false prophet gives "life" to this image (v. 15). The image is able to speak, so people think it is alive. This could be done by a false miracle which would produce a type of animation that looks lifelike. Since Christ alone has the gift of life (John 11:25), this image only appears to be alive. However, many think it is alive and fall down and worship it.

This false prophet also tries to force all people to bear a mark that shows their allegiance to the first beast.

This will be a difficult time for believers and many will be martyred because they will not receive the mark of the beast nor will they worship the beast or his image (Rev. 20:4). The mark of the beast (vv. 16-18) is for all people, small and great, rich and poor, free and slave. It has an economic purpose, for without it people are not able to buy or sell. This mark is visible, for it is placed on the forehead or on the right hand.

There are many "marks" being used by our society today which foreshadow such a mark as this. For example, we have area codes, zip codes, social security numbers, electronic banking, electronic price codes. People today are being prepared so that when they are asked to put on the mark of the beast, they will not question it.

What is the mark of the beast? The number is the number of

man, that is, 666. This number has been variously interpreted, but the best explanation is given in the text itself (v. 18). God says it is the number of man. As seven is the number of perfection (the world was created in seven days) and three is the number of the Trinity (there are three persons in the Trinity), so six is the number of man (man was created on the sixth day of creation). The Tribulation will be the day of man, the day when man is occupied with himself. The number of the beast will remind man of that.

The dragon, the Antichrist, the false prophet—these three persons will deceive the world during the Tribulation. They will seek to establish Satan's program on the earth. Together, they show us what will happen when Satan is allowed to pursue his own purposes. But one day, God will stop all of this and cast all three of these beings into the lake of fire.

How important it is for us to know that Satan can be defeated today! But victory over him is not with physical or material weapons. Rather, since we are in a spiritual war, we need spiritual power. We need the armor God has provided, and it is readily available (Eph. 6:10-18). We need the Lord first, and we need to allow Him to fight Satan for us. He will defeat Satan today, as one day He will defeat him permanently.

9
World
War III

(Revelation 14—16)

In the middle of one of the largest Air Force bases in the world, there is a very special room. Only those with the highest military clearance can enter that room. Across one entire wall is a large world map with models of military aircraft fastened to it. On the other side of the room are officers gathering schedules, military requirements, and weather information. This is the Air Force command room for military operations throughout the world.

In the center of the room sits the officer in charge, who by telephone directs the moment-to-moment Air Force military operations. As he directs, the model planes are physically moved by full-time airmen across the huge map on the wall. In an instant, one can see what is happening, militarily speaking, in any part of the world.

In the middle of the night a call is received in the command center from the Joint Chiefs of Staff. Immediately a crisis action team of key staff members is assembled. War plans are dusted off. Special briefings are given to the generals and their staffs.

"What will happen if there is an uprising in Indonesia?" a general asks. The officer in charge goes over the contingency plans in minute detail.

"What happens if there is trouble in Pakistan?" another general questions. Again a careful briefing is given.

"But what will happen if oil is shut off in the Middle East?" another asks. "What will we do if a ship is sunk in the Persian Gulf or the oil fields are invaded?"

What would we do? The world constantly stands at the brink of all-out war. In a day of relative peace, the possibility of war looms large, the potential is all around us. In the last three decades there have been at least 119 armed conflicts involving 69 nations, and anyone of them could have exploded into a holocaust.

According to the Scriptures, there will one day be another world war. Nations will be gathered together to fight one another, and one of the places where this war will be fought is called Armageddon. Blood there will flow four-and-one-half feet deep for the space of 200 miles (Rev. 14:20).

In the Book of Revelation, God shows exactly what will take place. In the midst of the final judgments poured out on the earth, the Lord unveils this world-devastating catastrophe. Before He does, however, He makes some important announcements of events that also will occur during the coming Tribulation. Notice carefully what He says.

The Announcements from Heaven [14:1-20]

Announcement of the 144,000 (14:1-5). In the opening portion of this chapter, the Apostle John again sees the Lamb on Mount Zion. This, as we have seen (5:6; 7:14-17; 13:8) is none other than Christ, the Lamb of God. Again He is standing to show His care and concern for His people.

With the Lamb are the 144,000, the ones first seen in Revelation 7. That the number is the same shows this is the same group, but here they are in heaven, whereas before they were on earth. They are before the throne in Mount Zion of heaven, the place where God dwells (cf. Heb. 12:22-23).

How are these people pictured here? Before, they were pictured as sealed servants of God, specially protected witnesses of the Lord on the earth. Now they are in heaven, singing a new song before the throne of God. This song of redemption is a testimony to the fact they have been purchased from the earth. Accompanied with harps, the 144,000 sing before other heavenly beings, the living creatures, and the elders.

An important characteristic of the 144,000 is their all-out service for God. They are "virgins" because they regarded their service for God to be more important than their physical relationships. If the Apostle Paul felt that such dedication was needed in his day (1 Cor. 7:26), will it not be needed even more during the Tribulation Period?

The 144,000 are the firstfruits to God and the Lamb (v. 4). In Israel, when the harvest began, the earliest gathered fruits, the firstfruits, were brought to the Lord and dedicated to Him. In the same way, Christ is the firstfruits of resurrection, the first One to be raised from the dead never to die again (1 Cor. 15:20). The 144,000 are the firstfruits of the Tribulation Period, the first ones saved during that time, although there will be a much larger group that will come to the Lord after them. There are many ways the 144,000 will be able to come to the Lord even though the church is gone. As we have seen, there still will be available recorded Gospel messages, Christian books, Gospel tracts, and the Scriptures themselves.

Another characteristic of the 144,000 is that they are blameless before God (v. 5). This does not mean they do not sin, but rather they are positionally perfect before God, and are living lives consistent with what they believe. In this way they also are witnesses for the Lord.

The 144,000 are therefore people who will be saved at the beginning of the Tribulation living separated lives of service unto God. They will be specially protected by God from physical danger. Their privilege will be leading others to the Saviour.

Although the 144,000 are not with us today, this passage should encourage us to witness for the Lord.

Announcement of the everlasting Gospel (vv. 6-8). John next sees another angel with an everlasting Gospel to preach (v. 6). What is the everlasting Gospel? The word *gospel* means "good news," and the context here shows what that good news is. It is the good news (to believers) that judgment is coming to those who live on the earth, "the hour of His judgment is come" (v. 7). This hour of judgment points to all the judgments described in the next two chapters, the bowl judgments. But there is still time to be saved; this is God's final call to an ungodly world to turn to Him.

Another angel announces a specific event of judgment, the fall of Babylon (v. 8). This proclamation points to Revelation 17 and 18, which describe in detail the fall of Babylon. Babylon falls because she has permeated all the nations with immorality. These verses introduce both the bowl judgments and the fall of Babylon, the subjects of the next four chapters.

Announcement of the beast worshipers (vv. 9-13). Next, John hears a third angel give a message concerning those who worship the beast and his image. What is this message?

First, it is a message of God's wrath (vv. 10-11). The anger of God will be poured out on the beast worshipers without mixture. Literally, it is a mixture unmixed, meaning they will receive the full force of God's wrath. It will not be watered down. God may delay His judgment, but He will not dilute it.

The evidence of such wrath is seen in the punishment of the beast worshipers. They are tormented with fire and brimstone. This is descriptive of the most potent punishment because brimstone is burning sulphur, a chemical that gives continual pain. Because of such torment they have no rest day or night (v. 11). The Lord must punish those who are against Him, since He is a God of holiness and righteousness. He has provided the way for salvation through the Lamb. If the beast worshipers do not accept the Lamb, they are tormented in His presence (v. 10).

Second, it is a message of encouragement (v. 12). What about the saints who have not bowed their knees to the beast? Is there any hope for them? In the midst of judgment, the Lord gives encouragement to those who continue to obey Him. These believers endure this time of persecution knowing that God will overcome their oppressors. God will punish their enemies.

Third, it is a message of blessing for those who die in the Lord (v. 13). Many at this time seek death rather than endure the torment associated with the judgments poured out on the earth. Rather than accept Christ as Saviour, they simply want to die. The angel declares that the blessing is for those who "die in the Lord," not just for those who die. God will reward those who die in the Lord. The deeds of their lives show their obedience to God, and God's blessing is theirs. What a contrast is their prospect compared to the judgment of the beast worshipers.

Announcement of the harvest (vv. 14-20). John next hears the announcement of the harvest that one day will come on the earth. How is that harvest described?

First, it is a ripe harvest (vv. 14-16). The apostle sees the One who will reap this harvest (v. 14). It is none other than Christ Himself. He is pictured sitting on a white cloud, which shows that He is coming from heaven. He has a golden crown (literally, a victor's crown), showing that He will conquer those who oppose Him. In His hand is a sickle, which is His instrument of judgment. He will cut off evil quickly when He comes.

The time for that judgment has come (v. 15). An angel announces that the harvest is ripe. Judgment can be delayed no longer. This is the time.

Second, it is a harvest of God's wrath (vv. 17-20). Although there is a great harvest in that day, it is a harvest of "the wrath of

God'' (v. 19), not a harvest of souls as it is today. This is the time when God's wrath is poured out on the earth, and the whole world is one great winepress with judgment pressed out by God. What exactly happens?

Several angels come as instruments of God's judgment. One angel has a sharp sickle (v. 17). The Lord Himself also has a sharp sickle (v. 14) and is the Judge in the ultimate sense. But He uses angels to help in accomplishing His purpose.

Another angel is one who has power over fire (v. 18). Some angels are specifically named in Scripture, but these angels are known by the work they do. This angel controls fire and uses it for God's purpose in judgment.

These angels work together. The angel of fire calls to the angel with the sickle to use his sickle. The reason is that the grapes are ripe, the time has come for judgment to fall.

Although God is a God of love, He is also a God of holiness and righteousness. As such, He must judge the world. He cannot condone sin and unrighteousness. He must deal with this earth, and the people upon it.

The angel puts his sickle into the earth, gathers the clusters from the vine, and casts them into the great winepress of the wrath of God (v. 19). In Israel today, laborers use great winepresses to press grapes. In that day, the whole earth will be cast into the winepress of the wrath of God. This is a picture of the great judgment that will come because the beast worshipers upon the earth follow Satan. This will result in the great world war, part of which will be fought in Armageddon, and all of which will be stopped by the return of Christ. The great devastation seen in these verses shows the futility of man's efforts as well as the necessity of God's judgment.

As a result of this judgment, blood flows up to the horses' bridles (about four-and-one-half to five feet deep) for a distance of 200 miles (v. 20). In that day and because of the war that comes, there is a whole river of blood. It flows for 200 miles or about the length of the land of Palestine today. The whole land of Palestine is one huge battlefield as the armies of the earth assemble there. But God will put in His sickle into this ripe harvest, and He will be victorious. Judgment is coming, and the Lord will win.

Introduction to the Bowl Judgments [15:1-8]

Revelation 6—19 describes the events on earth during the coming Tribulation Period. These are events of judgment, poured out by God on those dwelling on the earth. These judgments come in three series: the seal judgments (chap. 6), the trumpet judgments (chaps. 8—9), and the bowl judgments (chaps. 15—16). These judgments increase in severity as the Tribulation progresses. Chapter 15 is an introduction to the bowl judgments, which are described in chapter 16. Notice carefully this introduction.

The victors over the beast (15:1-4). John sees a "great and marvelous" sign in heaven (v. 1). In these next four chapters there are three great subjects: the great judgments (15—16), the great harlot (17), and the great city (18). This sign is "great" because the judgment soon will be over. The seven angels John sees are those with the seven final judgments, the bowl judgments. These judgments fill up, or complete, the wrath of God.

John next sees the victors over the beast, those who refused to worship him. These victors stand on a sea of glass and have harps of God (v. 2). They are victorious over the beast because of their faith in the Lord. They are commended for their stand and their victory over the Antichrist.

These victors sing a song of praise to the Lord for all He has done for them (vv. 3-4). As Moses gave praise to the Lord (Ex. 15), so do these servants. As the Lamb also gives praise (Ps. 22:22), so these servants give praise.

This song concerns the character of God, the One who is righteous, true, eternal. It is God who alone is able to judge the world. Such judgment is consistent with His person.

The temple of the tabernacle (vv. 5-8). In the Old Testament, Moses ministered in an earthly tabernacle. The Lord, however, ministers today (and in that day) in the heavenly tabernacle. It is this heavenly tabernacle, the Holy of Holies, that John sees opened, for it is the place of God (v. 5).

Who comes out of the temple? The seven angels, the ones with the seven final judgments of God (v. 6). Clothed in purity (clean and bright linen) and righteousness (golden girdles), the angels' judgments are righteous judgments from the Lord. They are given the judgments to be poured out on the earth (v. 7).

This introduction closes with the temple being filled with smoke from the glory of God and His power (v. 8). Judgment manifests who God is (His glory) and what He is able to do (His power). God must judge in order that the world may know of His holiness and greatness. The angels must now empty their judgments on the earth.

The Bowl Judgments [16:1-21]

The first bowl judgment (16:1-2). The first angel pours out on the earth the first bowl of God's wrath on the earth. This judgment contains loathsome and malignant sores which come on those who have the mark of the beast (all unbelievers) and who worship his image.

The second bowl judgment (v. 3). The second angel pours out a judgment on the waters of the earth that causes the sea to become like a dead person's blood. As a result, every living thing in the sea dies. Imagine the putrid odor caused by such a judgment!

The third bowl judgment (vv. 4-7). The third judgment poured out by the third angel is on the rivers and waters, which also become blood. Why do these unbelievers deserve to drink blood? Because they have shed the blood of saints and prophets (v. 6). They have persecuted God's people and therefore God must judge them. His judgment is consistent with His righteousness and holiness (vv. 5, 7).

The fourth bowl judgment (vv. 8-9). The fourth angel pours out his bowl of judgment on the sun and intensifies its heat. In a day when the sun is looked on as a great source of energy, it is important to realize that too much sun one day will be a judgment from God. Men will be scorched by the heat. What will happen as a result? Will people turn to the Lord? No. Instead, they will blaspheme the name of God and will not repent (v. 9). They will not change their minds about God nor give Him glory at all.

The fifth bowl judgment (vv. 10-11). Will the Antichrist be exempt from all of this judgment? Not at all, for the fifth angel pours out his judgment on the throne of the beast. When this happens, his kingdom becomes dark and the people gnaw their tongues in pain. This judgment produces physical torment throughout the entire kingdom of the beast.

The unbelievers' reaction, however, is not one of submission to God, but rather blaspheming the God of heaven. We see the hardness of men's hearts because in spite of all the judgments poured out on the earth, they do not repent of their deeds (v. 11).

The sixth bowl judgment (vv. 12-16). The next angel brings judgment on the great river Euphrates. This river runs across the northeast section of Lebanon, Syria, and Iraq down to the Persian Gulf. One day the river will be dried up to prepare the way for the kings of the east (v. 12).

Who are the kings of the east? We do not know specifically, but together they form a confederacy, for the word "kings" is plural. They are also from the east, that is, east of Israel. One day the Euphrates will be dried up so that these kings can come down into Israel as they march toward Armageddon.

At this point, John describes the gathering of the nations of the world for the great final campaign of God. He first sees that demons are used to gather the nations together. They come out of the mouths of the dragon, beast, and false prophet, the three satanic personages of the Tribulation Period (v. 13). These unclean spirits produce physical and spiritual immorality.

For what war are these nations gathered? Although this war is popularly called the battle of Armageddon, here it is called "the war of the great day of God, the Almighty" (v. 14). God brings this war to its end, for when He comes He puts down all war. Although it is Satan who instigates this war, it is God who allows it.

One of the places in Israel where this war will be fought is Armageddon (literally, the Hill of Megiddo). This place is located in northern Israel, halfway between Haifa and the Sea of Galilee, at the head of the plain of Esdraelon. A place of many Old Testament battles, as well as other battles throughout history, here the nations of the world turn their animosity against Christ when He comes to earth to set up His kingdom. But the Lord is victorious as He puts down all enemies under His feet.

The seventh bowl judgment (vv. 17-21). When the last angel pours out his bowl on the air, a voice from heaven says, "It is done" (v. 17). This seventh bowl judgment is the *final* judgment before the return of Christ. With this, the judgments are finished.

What is included in this judgment? It consists of widespread destruction and devastation. There is lightning, thunder, and a great earthquake (v. 18). Although there have been many earthquakes throughout the history of mankind this one is unprecedented. It is more intense than any that have preceded it.

The earthquake splits "the great city," either Babylon or Jerusalem, into three parts. In addition, many other cities fall (v. 19).

Islands and mountains are also affected (v. 20). Huge hailstones fall from God out of heaven (v. 21). These hailstones weigh about 100 pounds each. This final judgment from God is intense. In spite of this judgment, however, people continue to blaspheme God.

Immediately after the pouring out of this final judgment Christ returns to the earth to set up His kingdom. But before John describes that great event, there is one other episode that takes place during the Tribulation which he must relate. It is the destruction of the great harlot, and we will consider that next.

10
The
Great
Harlot

(Revelation 17—18)

At the edge of town, by the turn of the road, stands a stone structure built by the early settlers of the village. Painted pure white, it has a tall steeple with a mellow bell that still tolls once a week. Alongside is a cemetery that marks the history of the town; while inside the building is an ornate hand-carved pulpit, stained-glass windows, and worn, solid oak pews. When out-of-town guests are led by this building, they always ask, "Is this the church?"

On the west side of a large metropolitan city stands a brand new concrete and steel building carefully designed by a nationally known architect. "We wanted the latest for the people of this community," said the director of social concern. "We have a full-size gymnasium, game room, library, and complete athletic facilities. We still have a meeting here once a week with the pastoral staff, but we are interested in the physical welfare of our people, so we no longer preach a spiritual message. I guess this is why people often ask, 'Is this a church?'"

Nearby is the colonial red brick building where many people seem to live. Their children go there for youth meetings, Sunday

meetings, and Wednesday Bible study. Adults are there throughout the week and almost all day on Sunday. Their closest friends
congregate in that red brick building. People there show genuine
love and concern for one another and for others. They enjoy the
instruction they receive and the way they worship together. Recently one of them asked, "Is it the reality of Christ in our lives that
makes us a church?"

What is the church? Is it a building, a professing people, or a
group of genuine Christians? Is it a place with a steeple, a social
club, or a people vitally related to Christ?

Some may call the church building the church, although most
people understand it is only the place where the church meets.
Buildings come in different sizes and shapes depending on the
culture, community, and resources of the people. The early church
met in homes. Church buildings may come and go, but *the church*
continues.

Others believe all who profess a relationship to God are included
in what is called the church. This means that even those who have
lost all interest in spiritual things are numbered with true believers.
Whole churches may be characterized as professing churches. This
broad term for the church is sometimes called *Christendom*, that is,
all those who profess a relationship to God. Remember that Jesus
said the wheat and the tares, the possessing and professing, would
grow together in this age (Matt. 13:30).

Still others believe the church is the true church, that is, it
consists of only those in this age who know Christ as their personal
Saviour. United to one another throughout the world in a mystical
union with Christ as their Head, they meet together in local groups
for worship, instruction, fellowship, and evangelism. The local
groups are organized with leaders and regularly observe the ordi-
nances of the church as Christ commanded.

One day Christ is going to come and take the true church—those
who in this age have received Him as their Saviour—out of this

world to be with Him (1 Thes. 4:16-17). But the professing church, Christendom, will continue to be here on the earth. The question answered in this chapter is: "What will happen to the professing church during the Tribulation Period?"

The Religious System [17:1-18]

Its influence (17:1-4). The Apostle John sees one of the seven angels who had the seven bowl judgments. This angel tells him about the judgment of the great harlot (v. 1).

Why does God use the figure of a harlot to describe this system? During Old Testament times, Israel often worshiped idols, the gods of other nations. When Israel sought other gods, she left the one true God; she turned her back on the Lord. In other words, spiritual unfaithfulness is spiritual adultery; this is why the figure of a harlot is used. God describes a religious system which is spiritually unfaithful, a system that has turned its back on the Lord. This is an apostate or false religious system.

In several passages of the New Testament, we have prophecies about the professing church, or Christendom. We find that this visible church is characterized by progressive unbelief and apostasy. Such unbelief is to become more and more intense in the latter days (1 Tim. 4:1-2; 2 Tim. 3:1-5; 2 Peter 2:1-2; Rev. 2:20-23). Seen on the outside of the professing church, Christ stands at the door and knocks (Rev. 3:20). This professing, apostate church is unfaithful to the Lord and therefore described as a great harlot.

How widespread is the influence of this apostate church? First, its influence reaches the people of the earth. Notice that the harlot sits "upon many waters" (v. 1). Later, John identifies the waters as "peoples and multitudes and nations and tongues" (v. 15). This religious system is a popular movement, involving the whole world.

Second, the influence of the apostate church reaches the leaders of the earth. The kings of the earth are involved with this system

(v. 2). There is a horizontal relationship across cultures with the people of the earth. There is also a vertical relationship across classes with the leaders of the earth. All are involved with the sins of this harlot.

Third, the influence of the apostate church reaches to a confederacy of nations. Notice that the woman is sitting on a scarlet beast (v. 3). Is this not the exact same beast seen earlier in Revelation 13:1-10? It has 7 heads, 10 horns, and is full of blasphemy, which is the exact description as the previously mentioned beast (v. 3; cf. 13:1). This is none other than Antichrist, the leader of a 10-nation western confederacy.

Since the woman is sitting on the beast, several facts are evident. The woman and the beast may have a relationship, but they are not the same entity. The great harlot is not the Antichrist. Note also that the woman controls the beast, at least at first, since she is sitting on him. Also, the beast supports the woman, for he is under her. Perhaps this shows how the Antichrist is able to rise to power so quickly. Both he and the woman have the same interests, aims, and goals. With her blessing the Antichrist can quickly rise to power and become a world dictator.

Fourth, the influence of the apostate church reaches to the wealth of the world. The woman is clothed in all those things that show economic power: purple and scarlet clothing with gold, precious stones, and pearls (v. 4). The eventual loss of this wealth will one day be mourned by many throughout the world (cf. chap. 18).

Its identity (v. 5). What is this religious system? It is called "a mystery." The word *mystery* is a noun used here in apposition with the word *Babylon,* not an adjective which modifies it. In other words, this is not the city of Babylon on the Euphrates River, but rather a secret use of the word *Babylon*. It is the apostate church, a false religious system. As the true church is called a mystery (Eph. 5:32), so this false church is also a mystery.

How did this begin? The lineage of Babylon can be traced to Nimrod, the offspring of a grandson of Noah (Gen. 10:8-10). Independent Nimrod wanted to establish his own religious system by building the tower of Babel (Gen. 11). He tried to construct another way to God, rather than using the sacrificial system God had commanded. The Lord confounded man's language because Nimrod repudiated God's revelation and organized a false religious system. Representative of all false religious systems, this system was known as Babylon. Although the nation and city of Babylon were later destroyed, the religious system continued. It is a mystery Babylon that will be united against God and His purposes, a counterfeit religious system.

This system is not only identified as a mystery, but it is also a federation. The woman is called the Mother of Harlots (Rev. 17:5). Many groups join together in this false religious system, for they have a common bond of counterfeit worship. Their focus is on organizational unity. The oneness of which Christ spoke, however, will come about only through the unity of the true church, established by God for this age. Jesus said that unity, which was established on the Day of Pentecost, would be the same as the unity of the Godhead (John 17:22). The false church will never see that kind of relationship.

Its ingredients (vv. 6-15). The apostle further sees that this woman's purpose is to hinder, persecute, and destroy the purposes and people of God. She has martyred the saints and witnesses of Christ (v. 6).

Sometimes it is difficult to tell the difference between those who are true believers and those who are false. This is because the true at times may look bad and the false at times may look very good. Here there is no question that this religious system is evil, for it has martyred those who belong to the Lord. God, who cares especially for His own, must one day destroy this false system.

This religious system also has political implications, especially in relation to the beast. From where did this beast, the Antichrist, come? This is the beast that will ascend out of the abyss and one day go into perdition (v. 8). The seven heads are mountains on which the woman sits (v. 9). There are also seven kings, with the beast being the eighth (v. 11). These kings are a select group of Roman leaders with the eighth, the Antichrist, being the final leader, the leader of the revived Roman Empire.

What about that empire? It has 10 horns or kings (v. 12). Just as the beast Daniel saw had 10 horns (Dan. 7), so this empire has 10 kings or kingdoms. They will rule with the beast for a limited time and then give the beast their authority.

How will the beast gain authority over these other kingdoms? He could seize it, as other nations do when they take over a nation or empire. He could also be given it, as is true with a federation of nations. In this case, he is *given* power and authority (v. 13). This will be a 10-nation confederacy, ruled by the beast, and it could have many associate nations with it as well.

What will this revived empire, this confederacy of the beast, do? Its purpose will be to make war with the Lamb (v. 14). Since the beast is against God and the Lamb, his empire will be as well. He will be energized by Satan and seek to accomplish Satan's purposes. But will he win? The answer is clear. Instead of overcoming the Lamb, the Lamb will overcome him (v. 14). The Lamb will be victorious. The Lamb will win!

Its interruption (17:16-18). The Lamb will overcome the beast and his empire, but who will overcome the woman, the false religious system? What will happen to her?

The beast and his empire will overcome the woman and destroy her (v. 16). Why will he do this? Antichrist will hate this religious system. Although it is a false religious system, it does represent a professed relationship to God. The beast hates this. He wants to establish his own system of worship; he wants to put himself in the temple, call himself God, and be worshiped as God (2 Thes. 2:4).

He wants to have beast worship, not religious worship. So he will hate the harlot, destroy her (when she is of no further use to him), and take all the worship that would be hers for himself. Beast worship, not religious worship, will characterize the last half of the Tribulation, for the beast will destroy this false religious system.

From the larger perspective, however, it is God who will allow this to take place (v. 17). The Lord will permit the beast to destroy the false religious system and then the Lord will destroy the beast. When Christ comes to earth, He will take the beast and cast him into the lake of fire.

The Commercial System [18:1-24]

The fact of destruction (18:1-8). If the beast destroys the religious system to establish his own system of worship, what will happen to all the wealth the false religious system has accumulated? The beast (the leader of the political system) will destroy the religious system and take over the commercial system. Revelation 17 and 18 refer to different aspects of the same thing. Revelation 17 shows the destruction of the false religious system. Revelation 18 discusses the destruction of the commercial system after it is taken over by the beast.

It is a mighty angel, one with great authority, who announces the destruction of commercial Babylon. The angel says, "Fallen, fallen is Babylon the great!" (v. 2, NIV) Although this has been announced previously (14:8), it is described in this chapter.

This system now becomes the habitation of demons and demonic forces, because Satan is behind all of this. Both nations and kings are involved (v. 3). The merchants of the earth have gained great riches because of the false religious system.

What is the responsibility of believers who are living at the time of this false religious system? The answer is clear. They are to "come out of her" (v. 4), separating themselves from sin and all that is associated with sin. The sins of this system have reached even to heaven as an abomination against the Lord. Believers are to reward her as the system rewarded them—in other words, they should stay away from her and all that she has. She has glorified herself, has lived luxuriously, has thought only of self-indulgence. But now, plagues of death, mourning, and famine have come to her. And now it is too late. She is burned with fire, for it is God who judges her and destroys her (v. 8).

Mourning because of destruction (18:9-19). When the wealth of the apostate church is one day destroyed, what do the people of the earth think? They moan and groan, for the hopes of their lives are wrapped up in the things of this world. The kings of the earth cry out and lament because of her destruction (vv. 9-10). They cry because the system which looked so strong has fallen. In one hour, a short period of time, judgment has come.

The merchants of the earth also mourn for her (v. 11) because of the great wealth they see wasted. Gold, silver, precious stones, pearls, and fine linen depict economic prosperity (v. 12). This system has made the merchants of the world rich, but now all is gone. Those who put their hope and trust in the wealth of this world now have nothing.

The shippers of the earth also mourn the destruction of this commercial system (v. 17). Shipmasters, passengers, sailors, and all who make their living by the sea cry over her loss. They were made rich by transporting the great goods of this system, and now all of that is gone. That in which they have placed their hope has been destroyed.

Rejoicing because of destruction (18:20-24). If the people of the earth mourn the loss of this system, how do the people of heaven react? For them this is a time of rejoicing, for they see the judgment of God poured out on this system. Since God hates sin, those who love the Lord must hate sin too, and they rejoice over God's judgment of such a sinful system.

How will this Babylon be thrown down? A strong angel takes a great millstone and throws it into the sea (v. 21). The throwing down of Babylon will be like that; it will be with great violence.

Musicians, harpists, pipers, and trumpeters will no longer be found or heard in the city (v. 22). Neither will the light of her lamps shine any more, for her light will be extinguished (v. 23). The voice of the bridegroom and bride will not be heard there any longer. All cause for celebration will be ended.

What is the reason for such destruction? Because in her was found "the blood of prophets and of saints and of all that were slain upon the earth" (v. 24). This system destroyed God's messengers and so will be judged by God. God must punish all those who do not trust Him. Because of this, we see why it is so important to trust Him.

11
When
Christ
Returns
(Revelation 19—20)

The challenge was hard to refuse.

"I'd like you junior high students to read the Book of Revelation at one sitting," said the teacher. "We want to look carefully at the first chapter next week, but I want you to see what is in the *whole* book. Promise me that sometime this week you will get by yourself and read through the entire book."

Sarah never had read even a chapter of Scripture through all the way, let alone an entire book. And this Book of Revelation—what was in it anyway? But the teacher was very popular and had ways of checking up on the students, so Sarah thought she had better comply.

After Sunday dinner, Sarah excused herself and went up to her room. There she took out her Bible, turned to the last book, and began to read. The chapters seemed to fly by.

All of a sudden, as she came to the end of the book, she could hardly believe what she was reading. She read the chapter again and then called to her mother.

"Mother, Mother," she cried. "It's too good to be true."

"What do you mean, Sarah?" Mother asked.

"You see, Mother," explained Sarah, "this afternoon I've been reading the Book of Revelation. And Mother, I found out that we win! We win! We win!"

As believers, it is easy to be on the defensive, to become discouraged with witnessing and living for the Lord. But we need to keep our eyes on the future, on eternal values, on our Saviour. One day Christ will return to this earth to put all His enemies under His feet, to set up His kingdom, and to reign on the earth. And when He does, we will win!

The end of the Bible is vastly different from the beginning. In Genesis we have the creation of this world, the creation of man, and the beginning of sin. Sin has caused great havoc, great devastation, great pain and suffering. But at the end of the Bible, Christ is victorious over sin. He is victorious over Satan and his plans and purposes. Christ wins!

This is the message of Scripture, and it is especially the message of these chapters. Jesus Christ is coming again. And when He does, He will put down all enemies under His feet and of His kingdom there will be no end. Isn't it great to be on the winning side?

What, then, will happen when Jesus comes?

The Preparation for Christ's Return [19:1-10]

The praise to God (19:1-6). As the events of the Book of Revelation point to the return of Christ, praise breaks forth from a great multitude in heaven. Their voices ring out with the word *hallelujah,* meaning "praise the Lord" (v. 1).

The word *hallelujah* occurs many times in the Psalms where it is translated, "praise the Lord" (cf. Ps. 150:1, 6). In the New Testament, however, it occurs only four times, all of them in this passage (vv. 1, 3, 4, 6).

Why does this great multitude in heaven praise the Lord? Because His judgments are righteous and true (v. 2). Man judges on the basis of outward appearance, whereas God judges motives as well. Man's judgment is limited to what man can see; God's judgment is unlimited for He is omniscient. Man judges according to himself, his own standards and purposes, which are centered in man. God judges according to Himself, His own nature of righteousness and truth. This is why God's judgment is perfect.

Another reason for praise is that God has judged the great harlot (v. 2). This religious system which corrupted the earth and destroyed the servants of God has been brought down. When hallelujah is said the second time (v. 3), smoke rises up. This smoke is a result of the judgment of the harlot, for such smoke has been described previously (18:9, 18). God brings down all false systems, and such judgment issues in praise to Him.

Another reason for praise is because of God Himself, who He is as Sovereign of the universe. The 24 elders and 4 living creatures shout the third hallelujah as they fall down in worship before the Lord (v. 4). It is because of who He is that He is able to accomplish His purposes. These beings give praise because of His person.

All beings should praise the Lord, but especially His servants. This is why the command goes forth for His bond-servants—all who serve Him—to praise Him. In response to this command, a great multitude as the sound of many waters and mighty thunderings says the fourth hallelujah (v. 6). Why do they praise the Lord? Because of His coming reign, His kingship. The Almighty God one day will reign on the earth.

The marriage of the Lamb (19:7-10). In biblical times there were three stages to an oriental wedding. First, there was the betrothal, the time when the couple was engaged to be married. A very important event, the engagement lasted for a considerable period of time, at least a year. Mary and Joseph were betrothed (Matt. 1:18).

Second, there was the wedding itself, the marriage ceremony.

Third, there was the marriage celebration, the wedding reception. Jesus visited such a celebration at the wedding in Cana (John 2:1-11).

The church, in her relationship to Christ, will go through all three stages. First, she is now betrothed to Christ (2 Cor. 11:2). Second, she will one day be united to Christ when He comes for her (John 14:3; Rev. 19:7). Third, she will participate in a great celebration, the marriage supper of the Lamb (19:9). These last two stages are mentioned in this important passage.

At most weddings the bride is the center of attention, but at this one the attention centers on the Bridegroom, the Lamb (v. 7). The wedding garment of the bride is fine linen, symbolizing the righteous acts of the saints (v. 8). Today the Lord is preparing the bride for her place and one day she will be married to the Lamb.

There is also the marriage celebration, the marriage supper of the Lamb (v. 9). This is a time of great blessing.

The excitement John felt was evidenced in that he fell at the feet of the angel who told him these things (v. 10). Angels, however, are not to be worshiped. They are fellow servants of God who carry out His purposes. Worship is to be given only to God (Matt. 4:10), for He alone is worthy of our worship. This is why the angel rebukes John. The angel also tells John that the purpose of prophecy is to unveil the testimony of Jesus, to reveal who Jesus is.

The Second Coming of Christ [19:11-16]

His coming (19:11). All biblical history points to these verses, for it looks forward to the time when Christ will come to earth to set up His kingdom. John sees heaven open and a rider descending on a white horse. At Christ's ascension, the angel had said that Christ would return in the same way as He went (Acts 1:11). His return would be visible and it would be from heaven.

Why is Christ on a white horse? The horse is white to represent purity and also victory, for He will defeat His enemies when He comes. He is called Faithful and True. He is faithful in that He will do all He has promised. He is also true, in contrast to all false messiahs, all who have promised relief from oppression and failed. Christ will bring lasting relief and peace on the earth. He is also righteous. Although judges throughout history make judgments according to outward appearances, Christ will judge in righteousness and make righteous war. He will put all enemies under His feet.

His clothing (19:12-13). How does Christ appear as He comes to judge the world? His eyes are a flame of fire, piercing their objects with His omniscience and having a purifying effect. On His head are many kingly crowns, diadems. He comes not only as Judge, but also as King. He has a name that no one else knows, a particular description of Himself.

His clothing is a garment dipped in blood—blood that reminds us of the past, when He died for the sins of the world, and that looks to the future, when He puts down all enemies. His name is the Word of God, that is, the manifestation or revelation of God. He is God and will therefore reveal God to us.

His armies (19:14). Who are the armies who follow Him? They are on white horses and clothed with fine linen. Are not these the ones who are married to the Lamb? (cf. vv. 7-8) These armies are the church, who has been married to Christ, rewarded, and now returns with Christ when He comes to the earth.

His sword (19:15). Out of Christ's mouth comes a sharp sword, so He can smite the nations and then rule them with a rod of iron. Many people on earth will be united against Him when He comes. They will be unbelievers, who have sought their own way. But Christ is going to put down all opposition and rule the world in righteousness. He must smite these people in order to do this.

His name (19:16). What is the name of the One on the white horse? Notice that it is written on His clothing and on His thigh, the place of power. The name is "King of kings and Lord of lords."

He is King among all kings and Lord among all lords. During His kingdom others will rule with Him, but He will be unique, He will be the supreme authority.

The Results of Christ's Coming [19:17-21]

The armies of the earth destroyed (19:17-19). The scene changes from the return of Christ to what happens when He returns. On the earth the nations of the world gather to fight against one another (cf. Rev. 16:13-16). Just as they begin to do battle, however, Christ Himself returns. Now all the hatred and animosity they have for one another is turned toward the descending Christ from heaven. It is then that He stops this war and puts His enemies under His feet.

It is interesting that when Christ returns there is no great or prolonged battle between Him and the armies of the earth. Rather, He quickly overcomes them by the sword that goes forth out of His mouth. The devastation is so great that the fowls of the heavens are summoned to devour the bodies of those He has slain (vv. 17-18). Those mentioned include all the peoples of the earth, the kings, captains, mighty men, free and slave, small and great. Although the Antichrist, kings, and armies of the earth are gathered against Christ when He comes, He defeats all of them.

The beast and false prophet (19:20). It is at this time that the Antichrist and false prophet are taken and cast alive into the lake of fire. One thousand years later they will still be there (20:10). The rest of the wicked will be cast in later, but these two tormentors, who had such a prominent place during the Tribulation, are the first to be thrown into it.

The remainder of the people (19:21). The rest of the people that were gathered together for this battle are slain by the sword of the Lord. Instead of their flesh decaying, the birds will eat it. This is a horrible end for these people. But it shows that the wages of sin is death (Rom. 6:23).

The Kingdom of Christ [20:1-10]

The binding of Satan (20:1-3). Following the Tribulation Period, Christ ushers in His righteous kingdom, a 1,000 year reign on this earth. This 1,000 year time period is mentioned 6 times in Revelation 20:1-7.

It is during this 1,000 year reign that Satan is bound with a great chain and put into the abyss (the bottomless pit). A seal is placed on that pit so he cannot escape to deceive the nations anymore. There is no temptation from Satan during the 1,000 year reign of Christ; it is an age of righteousness. Christ reigns on the earth to demonstrate how this earth originally was meant to be ruled.

The resurrection of the saints (20:4-6). At the beginning of this millennial kingdom, there is a resurrection of Tribulation saints. These are the ones who were saved during the Tribulation and were martyred for the cause of Christ. They are the ones who did not worship the beast and who refused to receive his mark.

The wicked dead will not be raised until after the 1,000 year reign of Christ (v. 5). They remain dead until right before the Great White Throne judgment, when God raises them (20:13). Only believers enter the Millennium.

Jesus is the One who told us there were two kinds or types of resurrection: The first is the resurrection of life for those who have done good as God sees it, those who have trusted Christ as Saviour (John 5:28-29). This resurrection occurs in several stages (1 Cor. 15:23). Christ is the firstfruits (1 Cor. 15:23), then the church will be raised at the Rapture (1 Thes. 4:16). The Old Testament saints and Tribulation saints are raised after Christ returns to set up His kingdom (Dan. 12:1-2; Rev. 20:4). This is why all who have part in this first resurrection are blessed and holy (v. 6).

The second resurrection is the resurrection of damnation, the resurrection of all the wicked. It occurs all at once, right before the Great White Throne judgment at the end of the Millennium (v. 13).

The loosing of Satan (20:7-10). At the end of the 1,000 year reign of Christ, Satan is loosed out of his prison, the bottomless pit. Has he changed after 1,000 years? No indeed. He goes throughout the world to deceive those who have been born during the Millennium and have not received Christ as Saviour. God allows this in order to show the world that even with a perfect environment, there are those who will follow Satan if they are allowed to do so.

The Gog and Magog mentioned here (v. 8) are not the same as those mentioned in Ezekiel 38. The time is different and so are the results. This is the battle of Satan at the end of the Millennium.

In this battle, God destroys those who follow Satan with fire out of heaven (v. 9). Satan is then taken and cast into the lake of fire where the beast and false prophet already are (v. 10). The reason Satan is not judged at this time is because his judgment already occurred at the Cross (John 12:31; 16:11). Even though he has been judged, he needs yet to be punished. His punishment is to be cast into the lake of fire, where he will be forever.

The Great White Throne Judgment [20:11-15]

There are many important judgments in Scripture. This judgment of all the wicked occurs after the millennial reign of Christ.

The place (20:11). The place for this judgment is not on earth, nor is it in heaven. Rather, it is a place between heaven and earth, in which there is a Great White Throne. The throne is white to show the purity and righteousness of this judgment. All are there who have not accepted the Saviourhood of Christ.

The judgment (20:12-13). John sees all the wicked dead standing before the Lord. In this judgment God examines two sets of books. The first is the Book of Life, the book that contains the names of all who have accepted Christ as Saviour. None of these people have their names written there. None of them are believers. They are all unsaved.

The second set of books is books of their deeds. Why is God going to judge these people also by their works? Throughout history man has always believed that his own works will save him. But in this final judgment, God clearly shows that even by man's own standard, his works, he does not measure up to the righteousness required to enter God's heaven. Man's righteousness is as filthy rags (Isa. 64:6). Man can do nothing to merit salvation, so God casts all of these people into the lake of fire.

Death is the separation of the material part of man (the body) from the immaterial part. For the wicked, Hades is the place for that immaterial nature. This is why death and Hades give up the dead, the wicked dead, and all the wicked are raised and given eternal bodies (v. 13). God then judges all the wicked according to the Book of Life and the books of works, and finds them lacking.

The results (20:14-15). All of these people are cast into the lake of fire, the place of eternal torment. This is the second death, that is, eternal separation from God. What a prospect awaits all those who have not trusted Christ as Saviour! All will know God has put them there because He will stand as their Judge. How much better to know Him today as Saviour instead of facing Him as Judge when He condemns the wicked.

If such judgment awaits the wicked, what is it that awaits the saved? Where will they spend eternity?

12
There's a Great Day Coming

(Revelation 21—22)

"I had a fantastic home," said Bob as he talked with his college roommate. "Our house was all Dad could afford, but we had a lot of good family times. I especially remember the vacations we took together. We always did interesting things like cave trips, canoe trips, mountain climbing. The best part was that we were together."

Mike explained to the project engineer: "As much as I would like to help you, I just cannot stay. My company loaned me to you for this week, and I have enjoyed doing the work and living in this city. But tomorrow I go home, and I am really looking forward to that. One week away from my family is long enough."

"I hope both Richard and Dorothy come at the same time," Daniel confided to his wife. "Both of their families are tremendous, and it would be great to have them all here at once. I so much want to see my grandchildren again. I feel our home has expanded and expanded over the years."

Whether we are college students, husbands, or grandparents, the word "home" conjures up fond memories for many of us. We may think of a mother, a brother, or a grandchild and the wonderful times we have enjoyed. We may think of Christmas, a vacation, or being cared for when we were sick. The warmest feelings we enjoy are usually centered in our homes.

But where will our home be throughout eternity? If earthly homes are but inferior illustrations of our heavenly home, imagine how wonderful that future home will be! One day this present world will be destroyed by fire, and God will create a new heaven and earth. Coming down on that earth will be a beautiful city, the place where all the redeemed will live throughout eternity. Abraham looked for such a city, a city that had foundations and whose builder and maker was God (Heb. 11:10). Jesus, when He was here on earth, told believers He was going to prepare a special place for them (John 14:2). What will that city be like? How can such a place be described?

These last chapters of the Bible tell how an entire city is going to come down out of heaven, a place prepared as a bride prepares for her husband. This New Jerusalem will be the home of all believers throughout eternity. The apostle shines the spotlight on that great day and then voices a prayer for Christ to come quickly. What will our future home be like?

The New Heaven and Earth [21:1-2]

The fact of it (21:1). John's vision is now moved from the Millennium, the 1,000 year reign of Christ here on earth, to the eternal state, the time when there will be a *new* heaven and earth. One day this world will be destroyed by fire (2 Peter 3:10; cf. 1 John 2:17). When this happens, God will create a new heaven and earth that will last throughout eternity.

The word translated "new" means there will be a new *kind* of heaven and earth. The *quality* of the world will be different than the present one, for it will be eternal and also perfect. It will not be subject to sin, for God will have done away with sin. During this time there will be no more sea, so that land will cover the face of the earth.

The city of it (21:2). John also sees the New Jerusalem coming down from God out of heaven. This is a city made by God and exquisitely decorated by Him. The city is not called a bride, but rather is compared to a bride who is prepared for her husband on her wedding day. Since Christ promised to prepare this place for us (John 14:2-3), and since He has been gone for almost 2,000 years, there is no question that this is a fantastic place. It will be described later in this chapter.

The New Life [21:3-8]

Have you ever considered the question, *What is heaven really like?* First, it is a place, a beautiful place, perfectly decorated for us. But heaven is also a type of life. Although all who know Christ as Saviour are enjoying eternal life now, in that day we will have redeemed bodies and will be in a redeemed place. What kind of life will we enjoy in that day? Notice some important characteristics.

The host of God (21:3). In that day God will dwell with His people. Generally we think of heaven as the place where we will be with the Lord, and of course that is true. But it is also true that God will be dwelling with us. We will be the hosts and He will be our guest. Does this not show the grace of God throughout eternity?

The absence of pain (21:4). Life today is often accompanied by suffering, discouragement, and sorrow. Sometimes there is joy, but true joy comes in achieving those things that matter, things of eternal value. Since this present life of sin will be done away, and we will have redeemed bodies as well as redeemed natures, much that is associated with this life will also be removed. This includes tears, death, mourning, crying, and pain. The care that God shows in doing this is seen in His wiping away *every* tear (the word is singular). Every association with and result of sin will be gone, for we will exhibit a life of complete, unhindered redemption.

All things new (21:5). Life in that day is characterized not only by the absence of suffering, but also by the addition of many new things. These include the new heaven and earth and the New Jerusalem, and all other things that surround the believer in that day. We will have new interests and new perspectives. The certainty of this is in His own Word.

Complete satisfaction (21:6). During this time God will freely give to those who thirst the water of life. He will satisfy their every need. He will give abundant life to all.

A divine inheritance (21:7). Because of God's relationship to the believer, he will *inherit* these things. God, who owns all things and has all things, will completely satisfy the believer. Although believers are adopted by God today and are His children (Gal. 4:5-7), throughout eternity this relationship will be evidenced to us.

The absence of unbelievers (21:8). During this time there will be a permanent separation of unbelievers from believers. Unbelievers will not partake of the blessings of believers but will be tormented in the lake of fire.

Those who are unsaved practice sins like murder, immorality, sorcery, idolatry, and lying as a way of life. In this chapter, God is talking about people whose characters are wrapped up in these sins. The unbelievers will be punished forever. This is the second death, that is, eternal separation from God. In contrast, believers will live with God forever and enjoy the blessings provided by Him.

The New Jerusalem [21:9-22:5]

Its people. The New Jerusalem is the heavenly city that John sees coming down out of heaven. Who are the people that will live in this city?

This beautiful city will hold the redeemed people of all the ages. This is described in another passage in which several groups are said to be in that heavenly city (Heb. 12:22-24). These include: (1) an innumerable company of angels, (2) the church, (3) God, (4) Old Testament saints, called the spirits of just men made perfect, and (5) Jesus, the Mediator of the New Covenant.

Its appearance. This city will come down from God out of heaven *after* the creation of the new heaven and earth, for that is the chronology presented earlier (21:1-2). It is possible that this city may appear during the eternal state, or during the Millennium, the 1,000 year reign of Christ on earth.

Notice that there are leaves in this city for the healing of nations (22:2). Such healing would not be necessary during the eternal state, but would be necessary during the Millennium, since there would be people living in natural bodies during that time. Notice also that it will not be possible for any unbeliever to enter it (21:27). During the Millennium, when there will be people born in sin, some of whom will not accept Christ as Saviour, this city will need to be guarded against them.

If this city appears during the Millennium, it will be the place for those to live who have glorified bodies, while those with natural bodies will live on the earth. Of course, Jesus did live on the earth for 40 days after He had a resurrection body, so that really is no problem. If the New Jerusalem appears during the Millennium, it may hover over the old city of Jerusalem. We know that Jerusalem will be the center of the Messiah's kingdom and the nations of the earth will go up to it (Isa. 2:1-4; Micah 4:1-3). The heavenly city will then be taken up while God destroys this world and creates the new heaven and earth. The New Jerusalem will then be brought down on the new earth. This passage (21:9—22:5), however, is discussing the city itself, not *when* the city appears. There is a big difference.

Its glory (21:9-11). One of the seven angels shows John the heavenly city. The city's overall beauty is marked with the glory of God. Although man has often wanted to see the glory of God, because of his sinful state, he has never been able to stand in the full blaze of God's glory. This was true of Moses, and also of the disciples on the Mount of Transfiguration. One day, however, in our redeemed state, believers will dwell in a city marked by the glory of the Lord.

Its security (21:12-14). This city has a great wall with gates and foundations. The wall has 12 gates named for the 12 tribes of the sons of Israel, and 12 foundation stones bearing the names of the 12 apostles. Israel and the church are distinct, yet together throughout eternity.

Its size and shape (21:15-16). How large is this city? The city is carefully measured and found to be 12,000 furlongs or 1,500 miles in its length, breadth, and height. This is a very large city, extending in one direction the distance of half-way across the United States. Of course, it has to be large, since it will hold the redeemed of all the ages.

The length, width, and height of the city are equal. There are two geometric figures that fit that description. One is a cube in which the length, width, and height are equal. The other geometric figure that could be a possibility is a pyramid. Although either a cube or pyramid shape is possible, a pyramid would more easily lend itself to the river of life winding down through the city from the throne of God (22:1).

Its materials (21:17-21). God gives a list of the stones that are used as the building materials of this city. Such a list occurs in three places throughout Scripture. One is the covering Satan had in heaven before he fell (Ezek. 28:13); the second relates to Israel during the Millennium (Isa. 54:11-12); and the third is here. Of the three lists, this one is the most extensive. God says that our eternal abode will be more beautiful than what Satan had before he fell or what Israel will have during the Millennium.

Of special interest are the gates, for each gate is made of a single pearl (v. 21). This shows the beauty and perfection God will display in the make up of this city.

The street is pure gold like transparent glass (v. 21). The word *street* is literally the "open place," that is, the broad space. In other words, this is a reference not just to the roadways of the city, but to all the city's open space. In our modern cities there are malls and openings between buildings, so in this city all the open space will be of gold.

The gold described here is pure gold like transparent glass. Today, it is impossible to refine gold perfectly. When gold is refined, the impurity in the gold gives it its color. If gold could be refined completely so that it would contain no impurities at all, it well could be as transparent as glass.

Its temple (21:22). Nowhere in this city will there be a temple or place where the citizens can come to worship God. Instead, God and the Lamb both will be in the city and will be the temple of it. We will not need a special place to worship, for we will be able to worship God directly.

Its light (21:23). No external light will be needed to illuminate the city. The glory of God and the Lamb will illuminate the city. This does not necessarily mean that there will be no sun or moon, but rather that such light will not be needed.

The nations (21:24-27). The nations will also be able to walk by the light of the city. The gates will not need to be shut since there will be no night there. Nothing will be able to enter the city that would defile it. It will be a perfect city for God's redeemed people.

Its river (22:1-2). In this city there will be a beautiful river, the river of the water of life. It will flow from the throne of God down through the city. There will be no pollution, for the river will be clear as crystal. On each side of the river will be the tree of life with different kinds of fruit. The leaves of the tree will be used for the healing of the nations, probably during the Millennium.

Its life (22:3-5). In this eternal city there will no longer be any curse of sin. Christ is victorious over sin and in this place the curse will be completely lifted.

This city will also be the place for the throne of God and the Lamb. It is the place where they will dwell and rule forever.

The servants of God will also serve Him there. Although believers today would like to serve the Lord, often they are hindered from doing so. In that day there will be no hindrances. They will be able to do all He commands.

Believers will also be able to see His face, the face of the Lamb. His name will be on their foreheads, a reminder that they are His, that they belong to Him because He redeemed them.

There will be nothing there to remind God's people of their former condition. There will be no night there at all (v. 5). Rather, the Lord will illumine them. He will be their Source of light. And what will they be doing? They will be reigning with Him forever. What a place, what a Person, what a prospect awaits all who know the Lord!

The Promises of Christ [22:6-21]

As the Book of Revelation closes, so does the Bible, for this is the last chapter of Scripture. It is an epilogue, a conclusion to the entire book.

In this final section, Jesus promises three times that He is coming (vv. 7, 12, 20). We should not only rejoice in this great assurance, but we should also be prepared for His coming.

His coming produces purity (22:6-11). In these verses, Jesus says that when He comes there will be blessings for those who have obeyed the words of this book (v. 7). He reminds His people that they are to live pure and godly lives in the light of His coming. He may come at any time for them, and then the Tribulation will begin on the earth.

What is John's reaction to this? It is such wonderful news that he again falls down to worship the angel who showed him these things (v. 8). But John is wrong. Angels are fellow-servants and are not to be worshiped. The only One we are to worship is God Himself.

The message is that we should be working and doing the Lord's will today in light of His coming for us. This is why this message should not be sealed (v. 10). The time of the Lord's coming is near.

This life determines where we will spend eternity. Those who accept Christ as their Saviour will spend eternity with Him. But those who reject Him will continue to be unrighteous forever (v. 11). There is no second chance, there is nothing that can change where we will spend eternity.

His coming produces rewards (22:12-19). Jesus promises that when He comes, He will reward believers. He is in control of all things and He will give rewards to all who have been faithful to Him. Those who have done His commandments will have the right to the tree of life and will enter the New Jerusalem (v. 14). Unbelievers will be "outside," cut off from Him (v. 15).

Christ alone is the One who will inherit David's throne; He is the bright morning Star (v. 16). This is why He is able to give such a gracious invitation to "come" (v. 17). This is the last such invitation in the Bible.

There is a special warning to any who would add to or remove anything from this book. Such a person will receive the plagues of God as a special punishment for tampering with God's message to us. The Scriptures are the very words of God and are not to be manipulated by man.

His coming is certain (22:20-21). Although many signs of the Tribulation and events of the future are mentioned in this great book, the believer should not be looking for such signs. Rather we are to be looking for our Saviour. His coming is certain, and He is coming quickly for us. Our prayer should be that He might come at any time, for we long to be with Him and want Him to take us home. But while we are here, we need to be serving Him and doing

His will until He comes. This is why we need "the grace of the Lord Jesus" with which this book closes.

Let us pray with the apostle, "Come, Lord Jesus" (v. 20).